Flower Coloring Books for Adults

Coloring Books for Adults Creative Coloring Inspirations

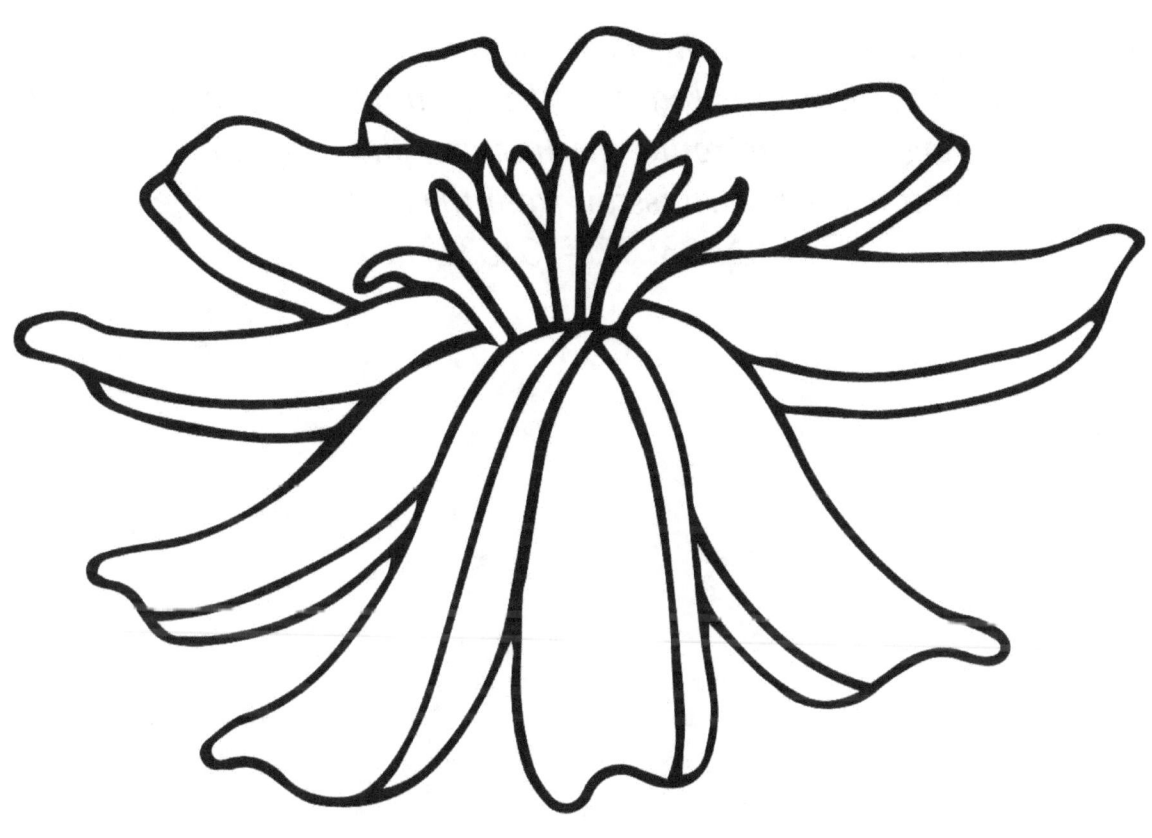

By

Jacob Kaiwell

Published by PUBLISHING COMPANY in 2015
First edition: First printing
Illustrations and design © 2015 Jacob Kaiwell

allcoloringbook.com
Follow me at fan page kaiwellcoloringbooks

ISBN-13: 978-1515317081

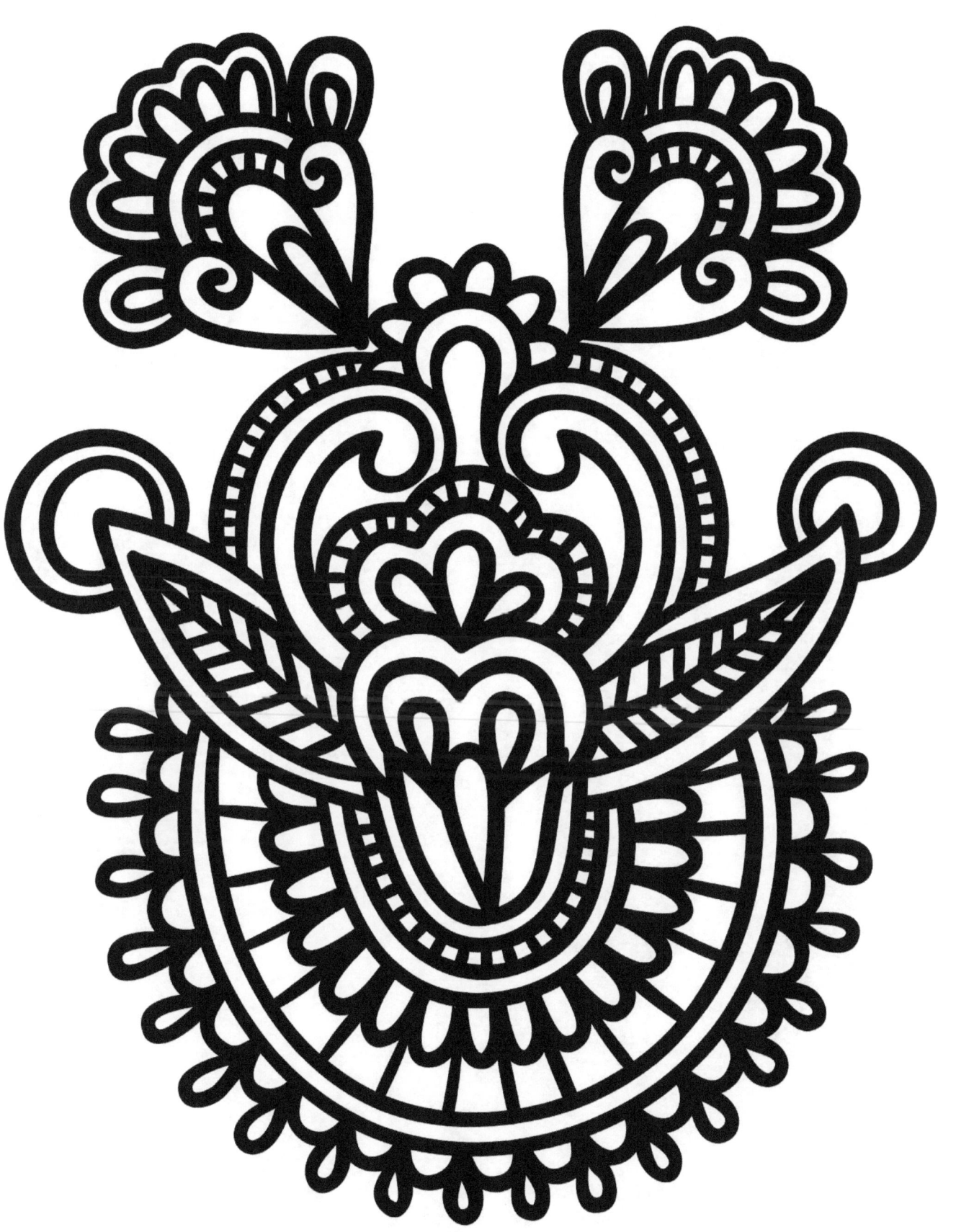

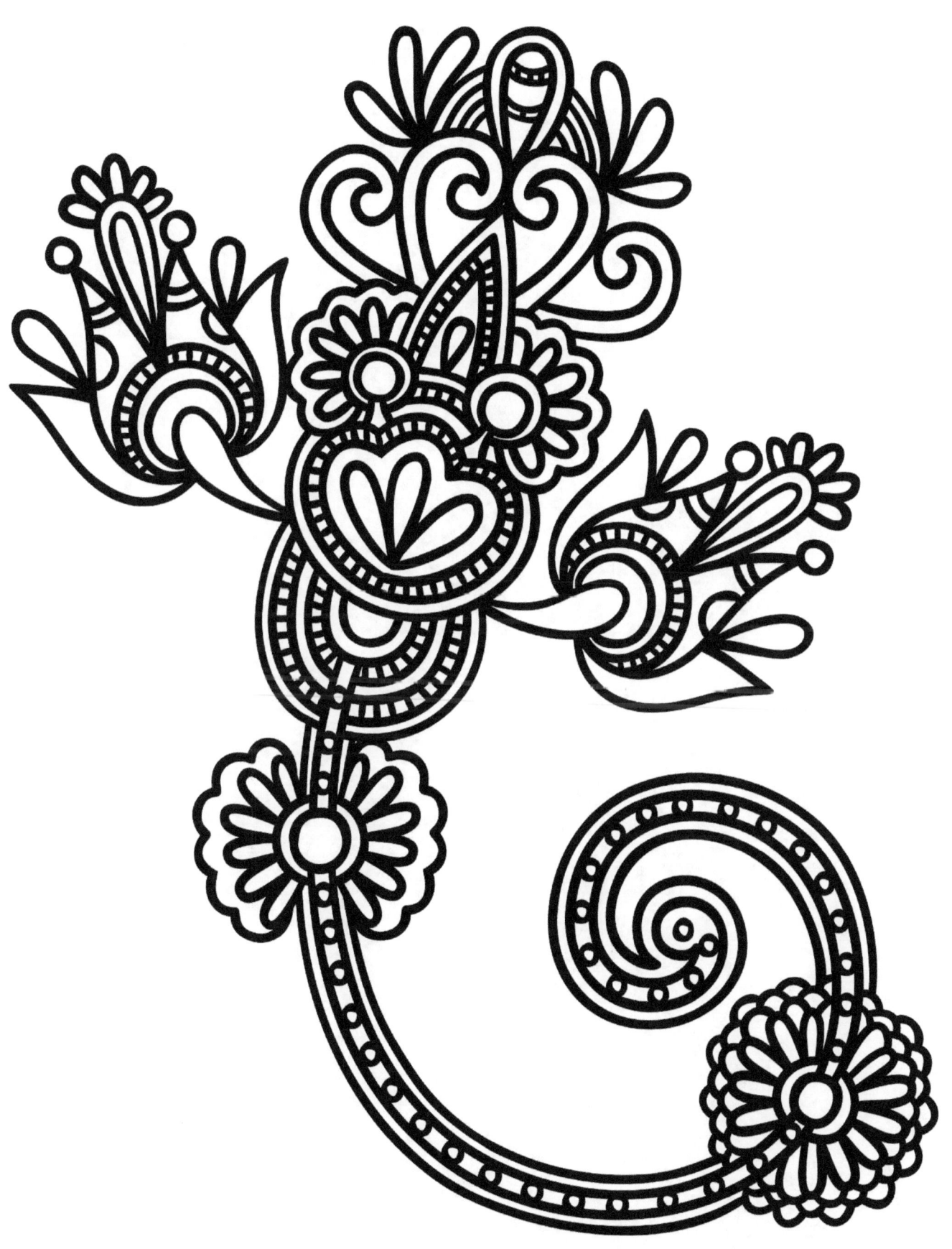

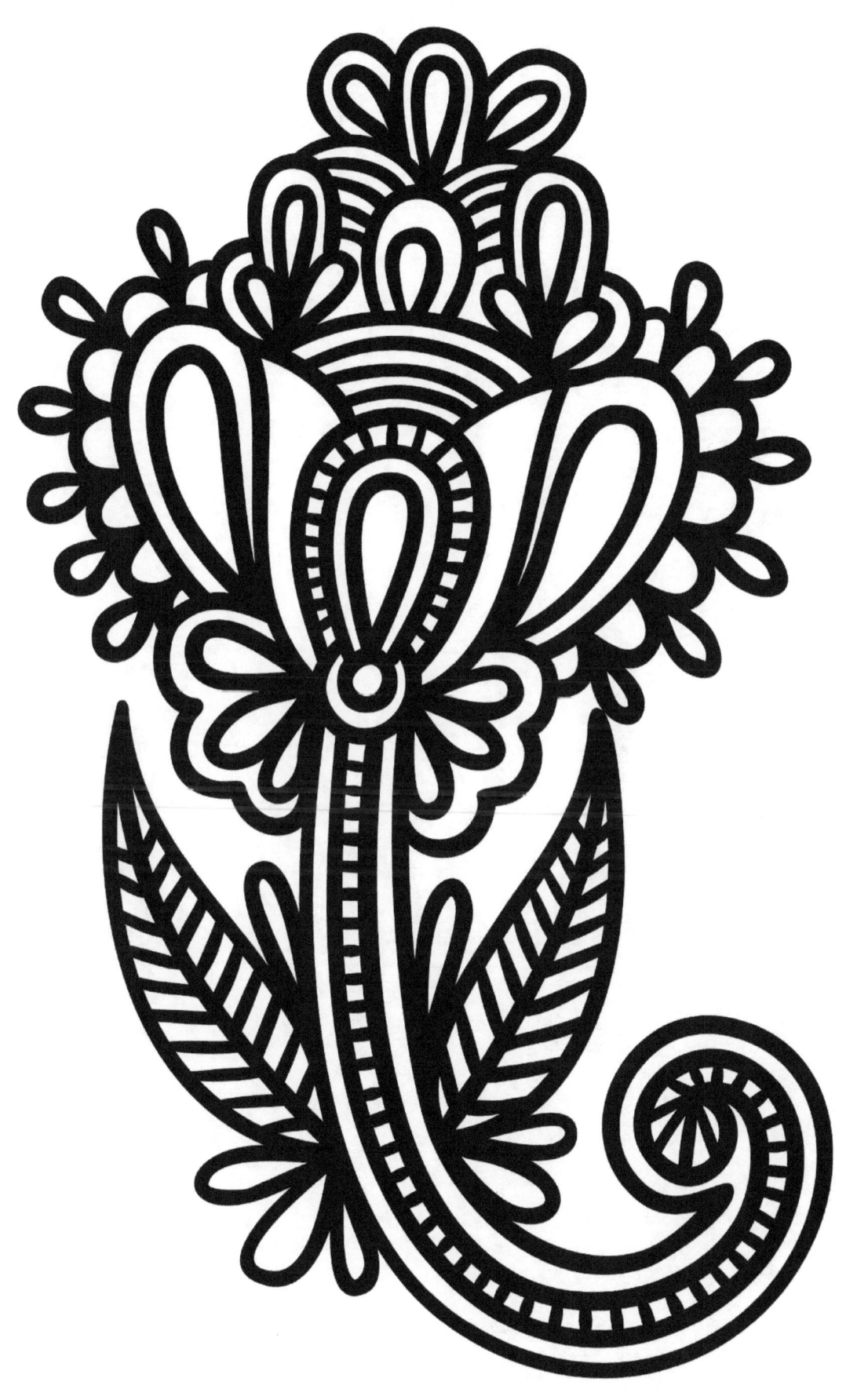

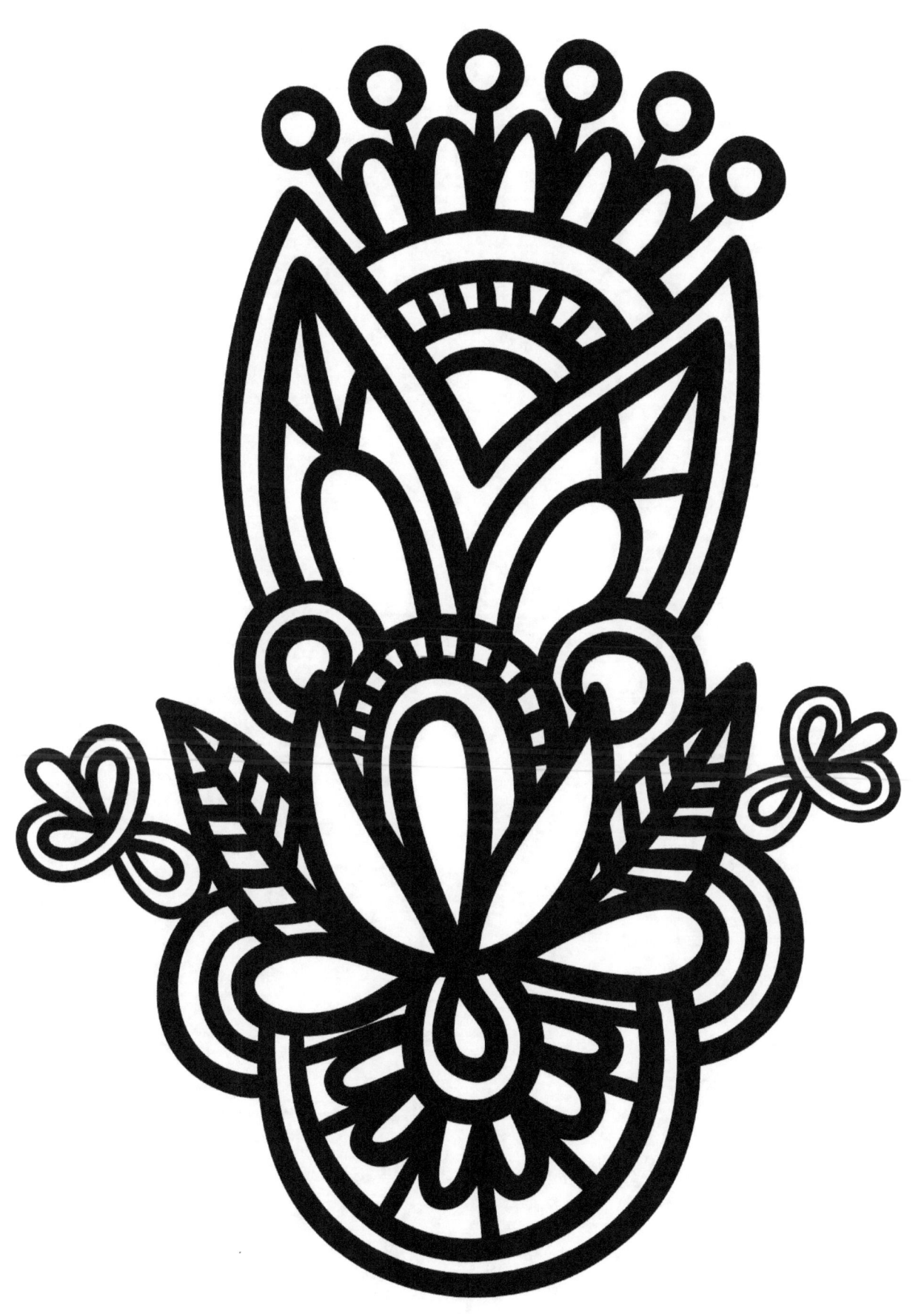

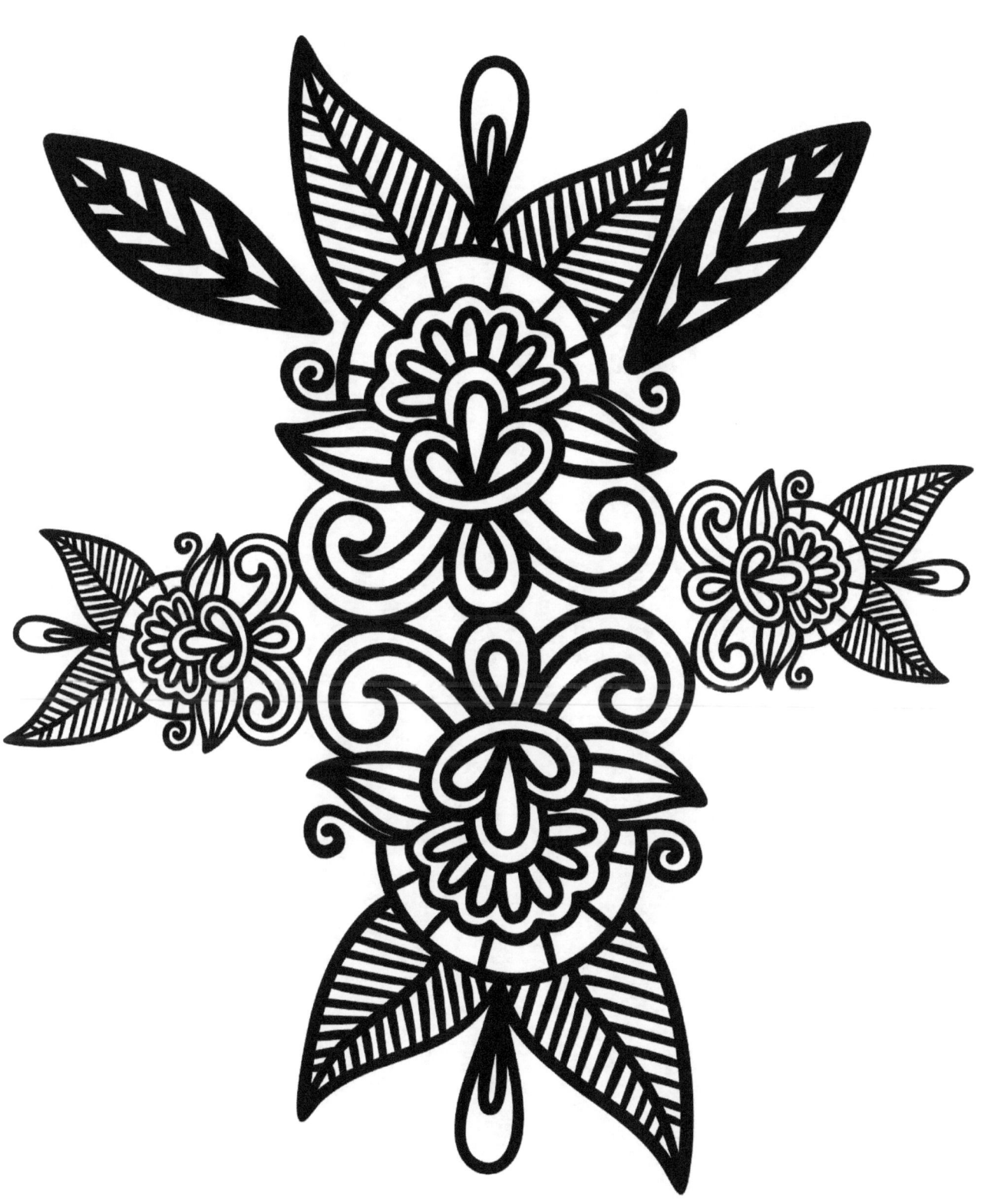

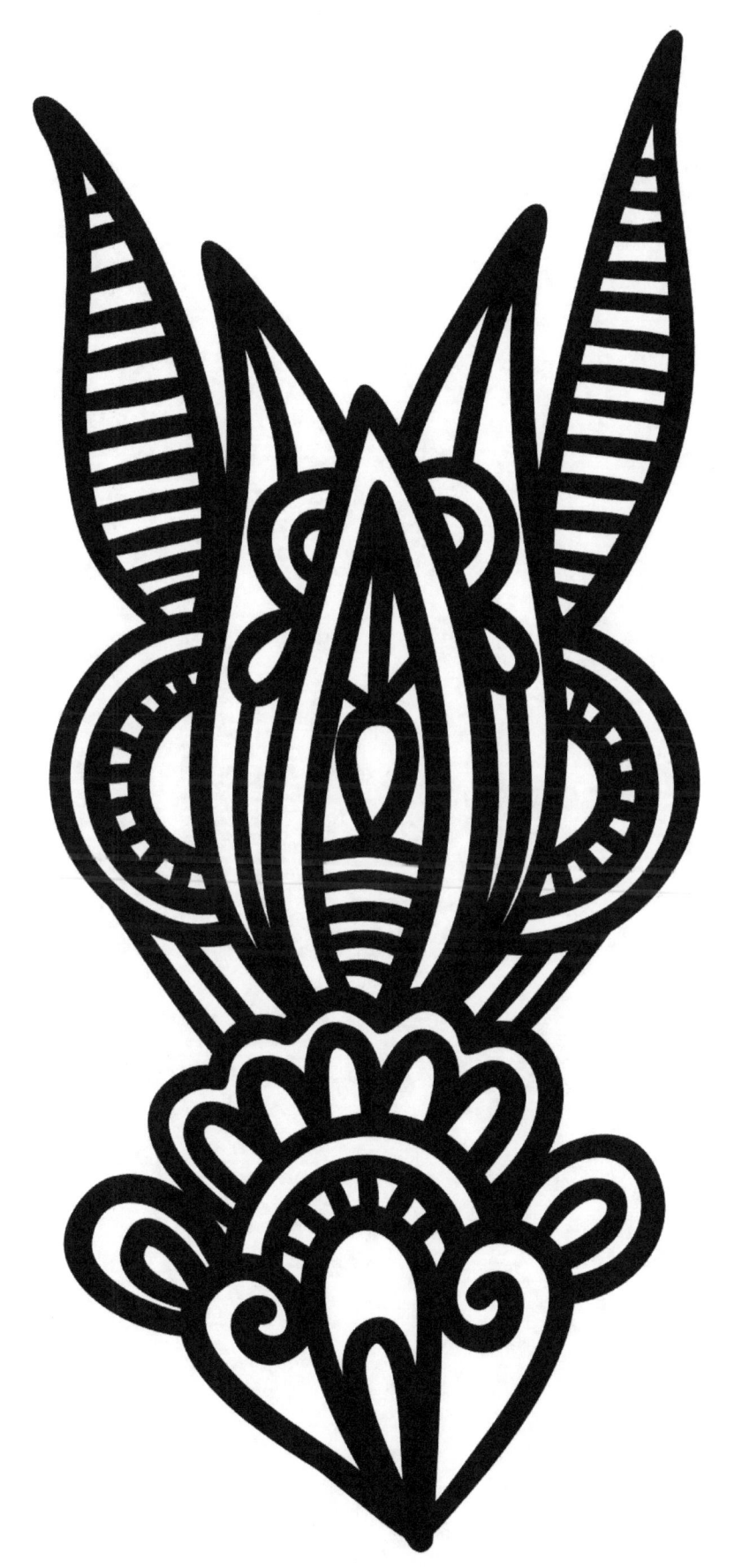

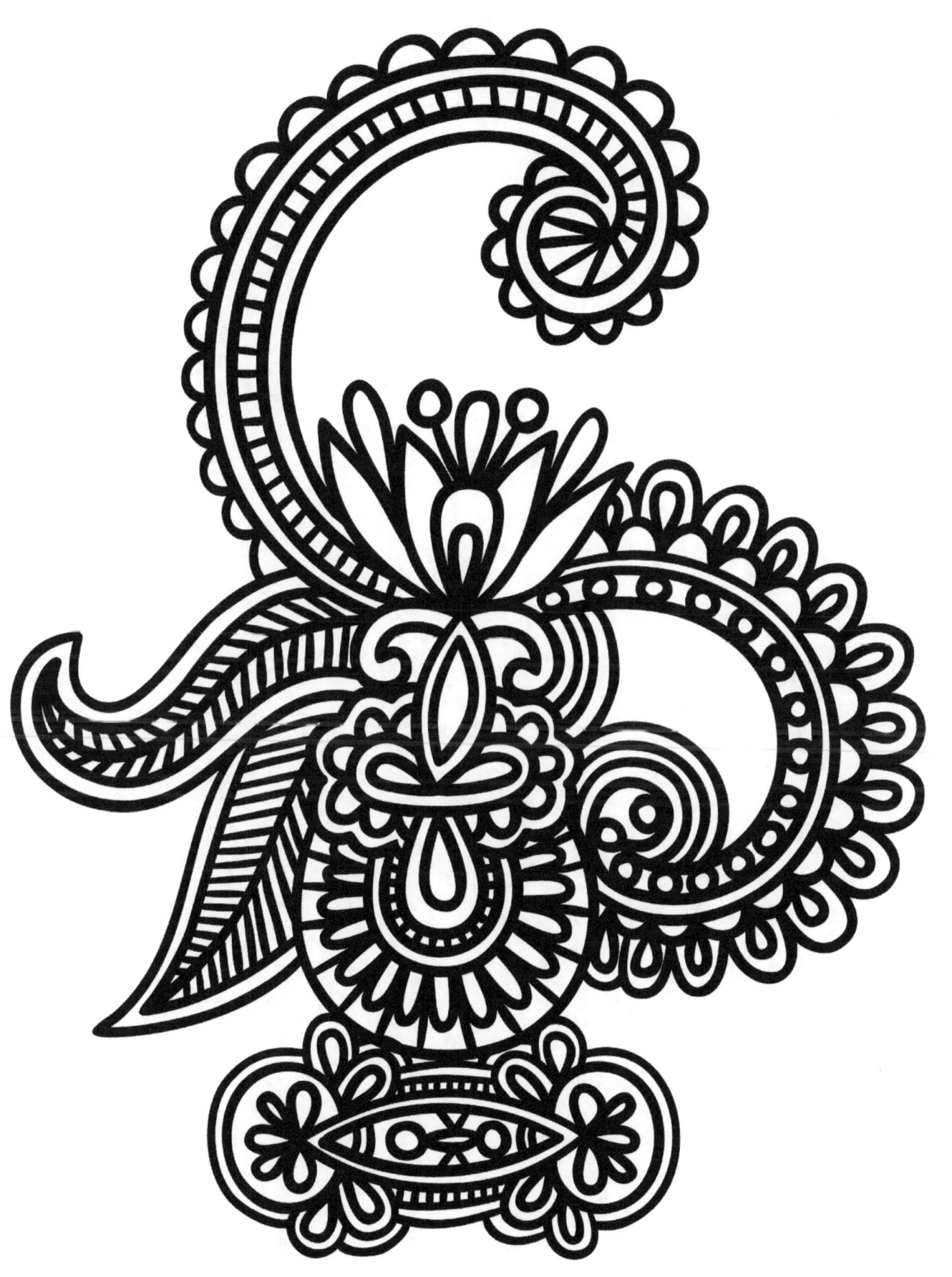

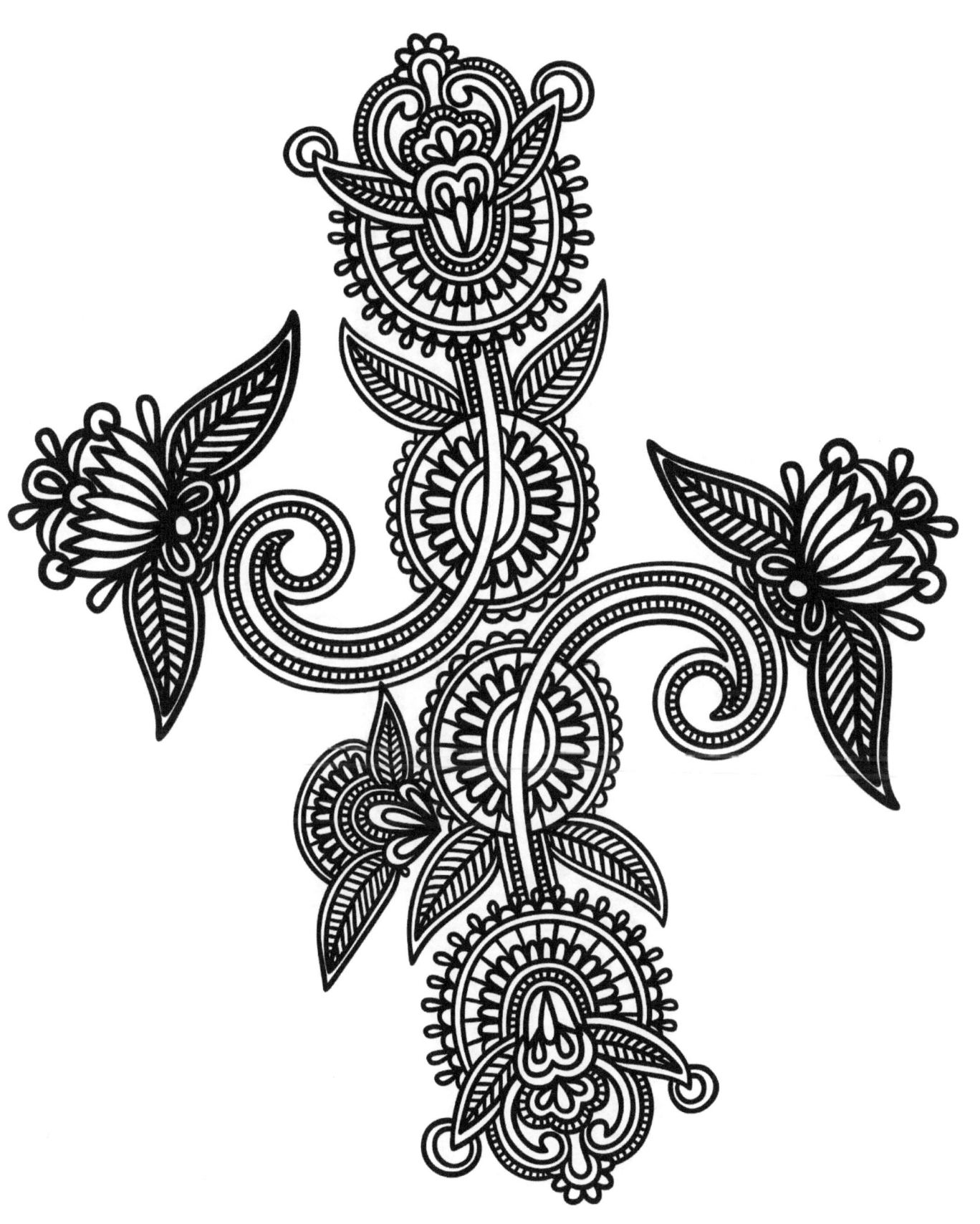

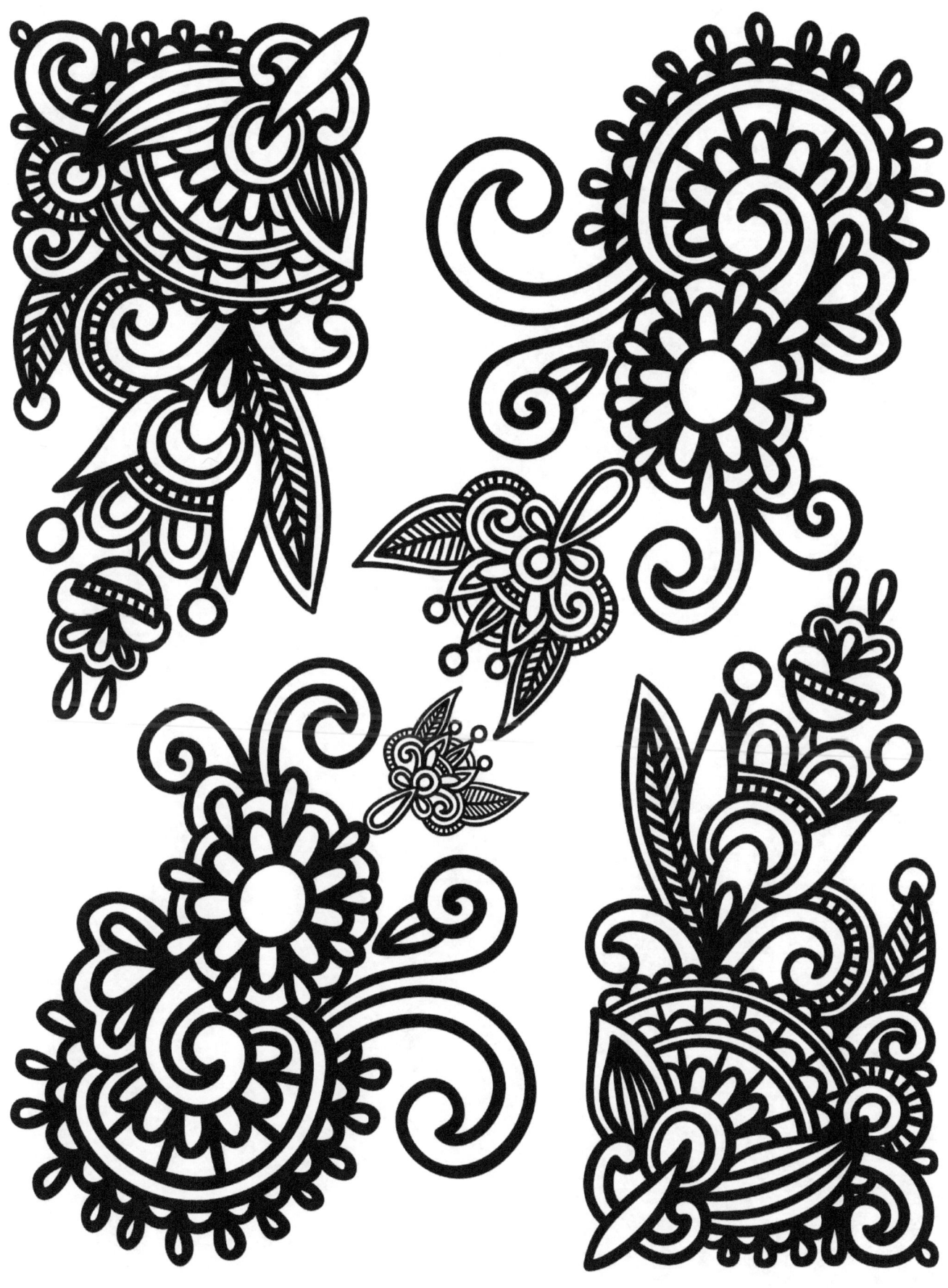

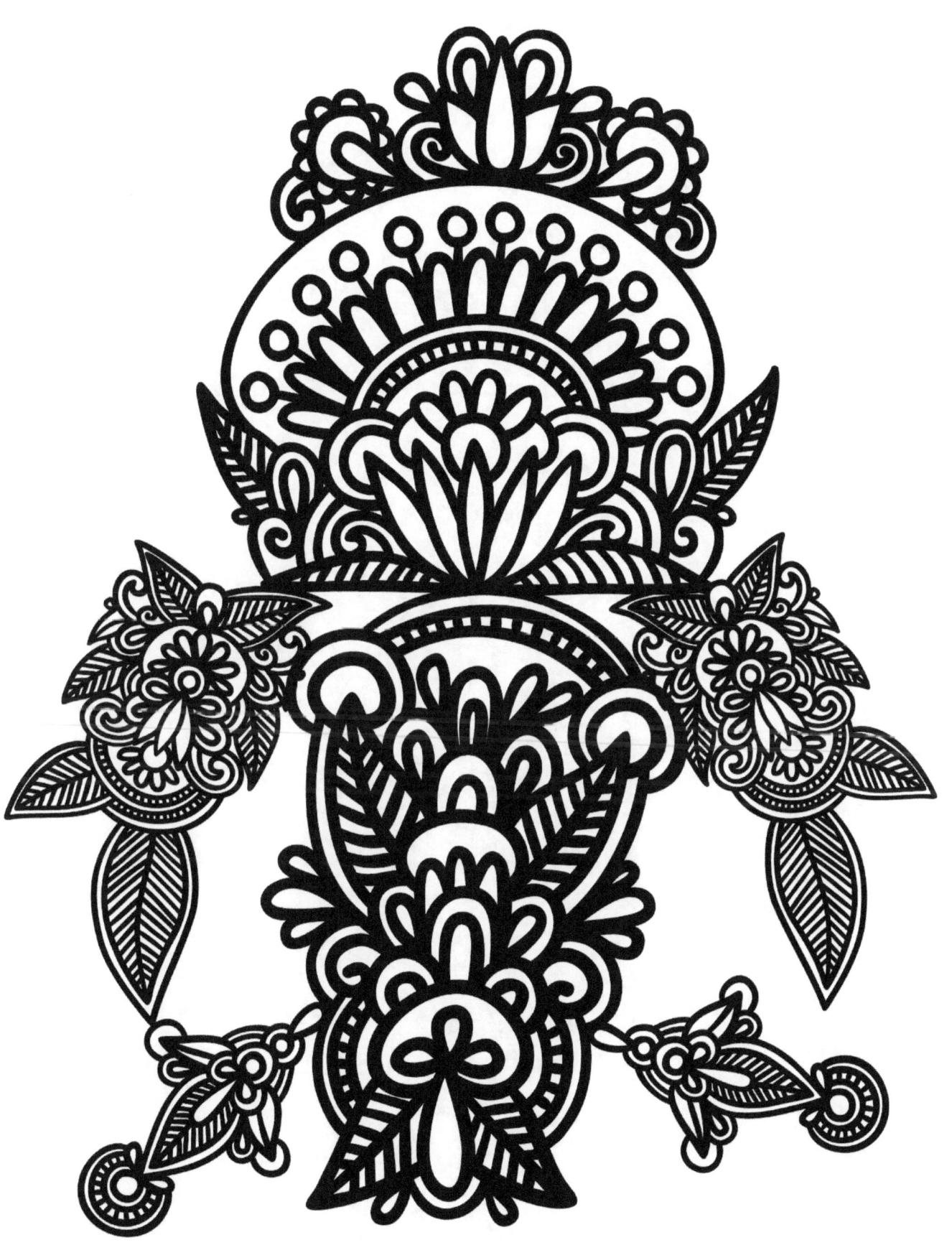

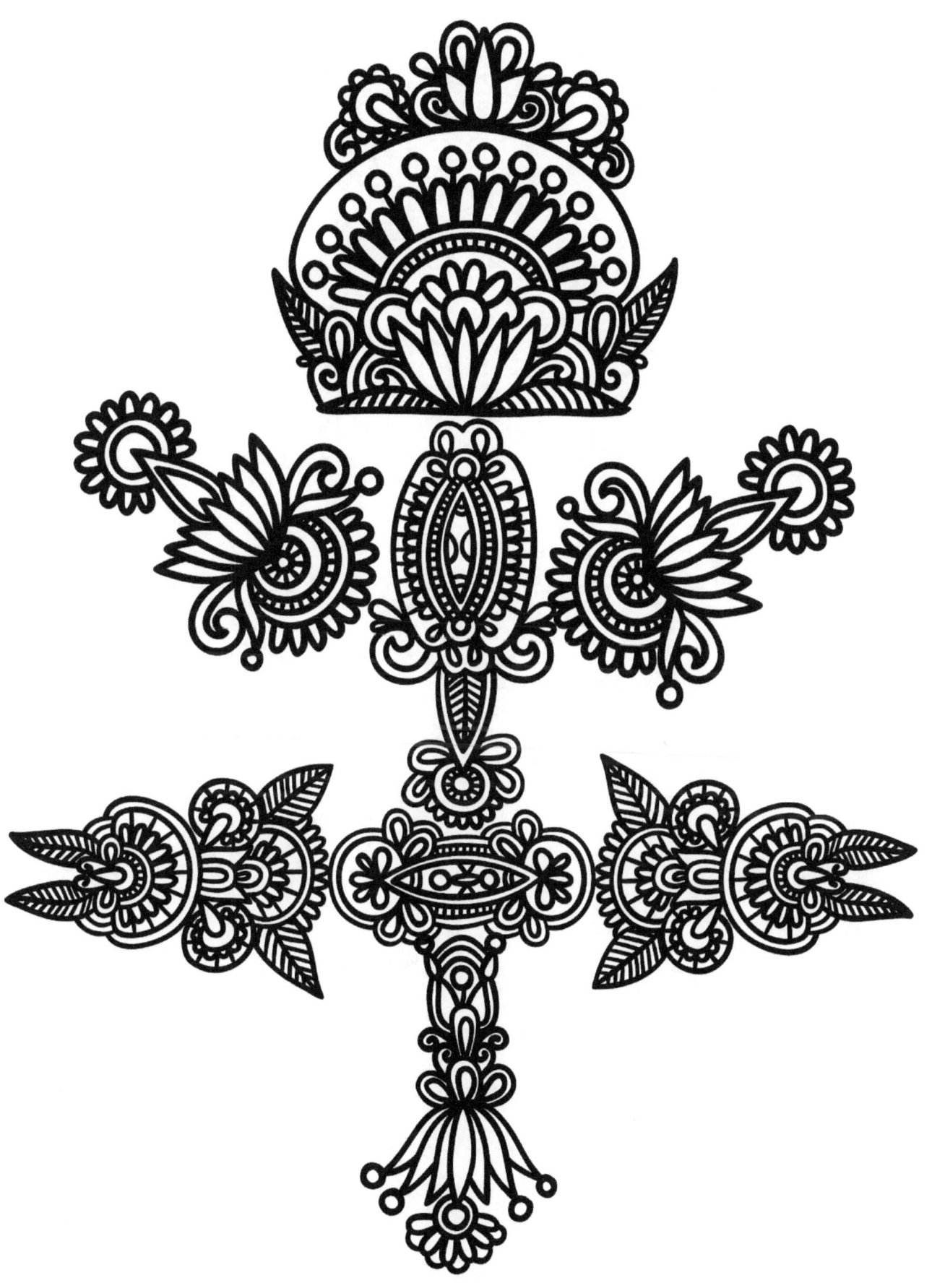

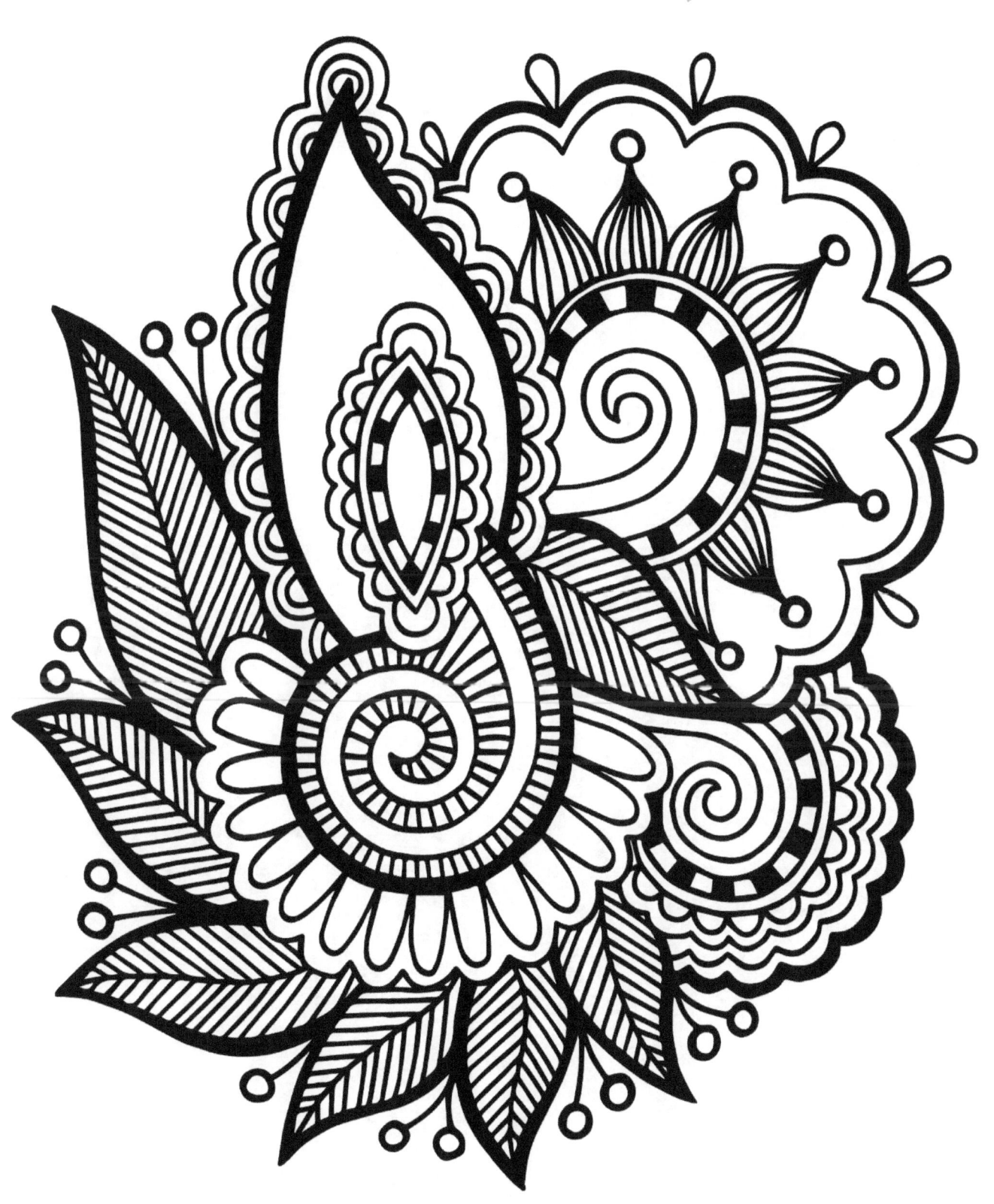

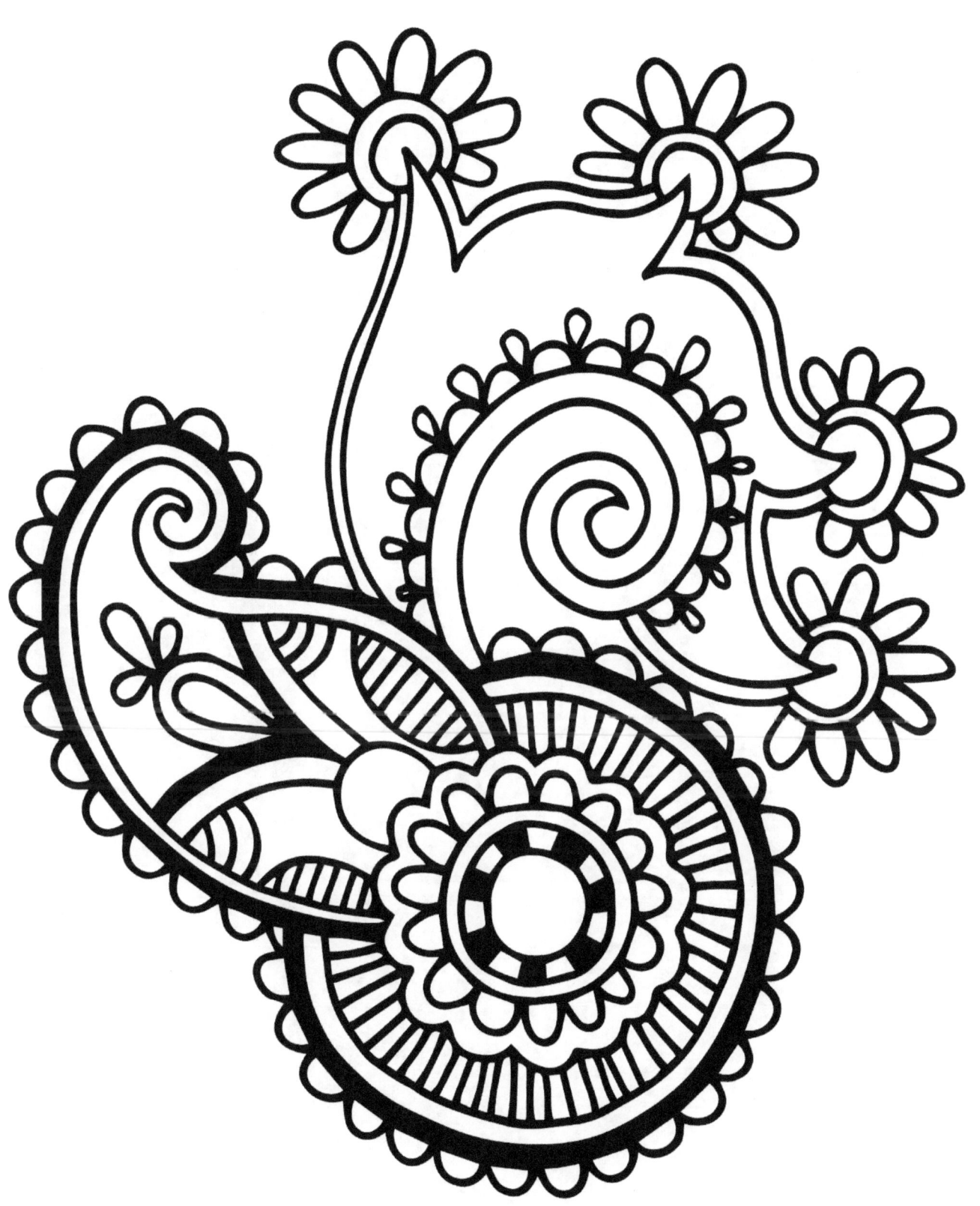

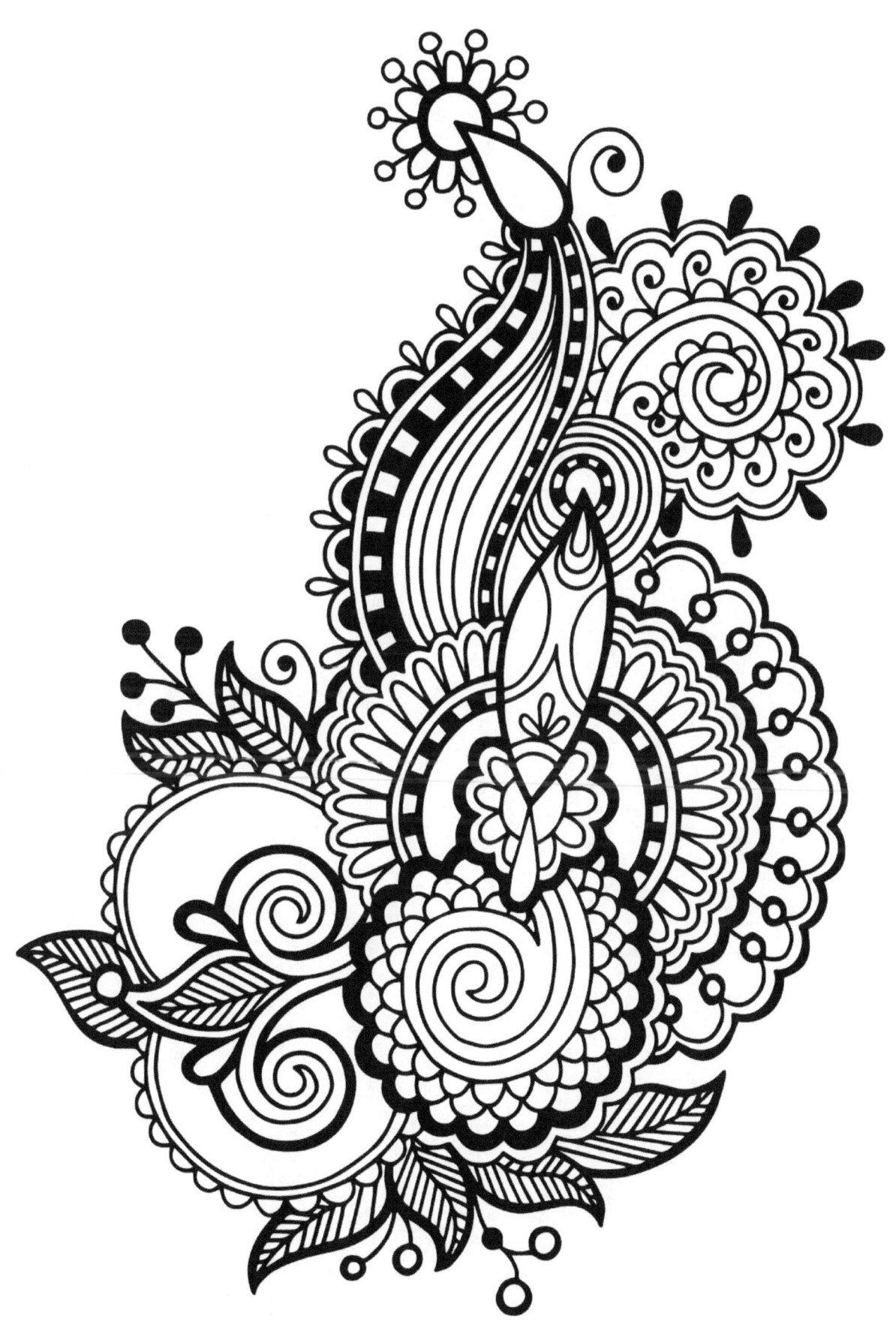

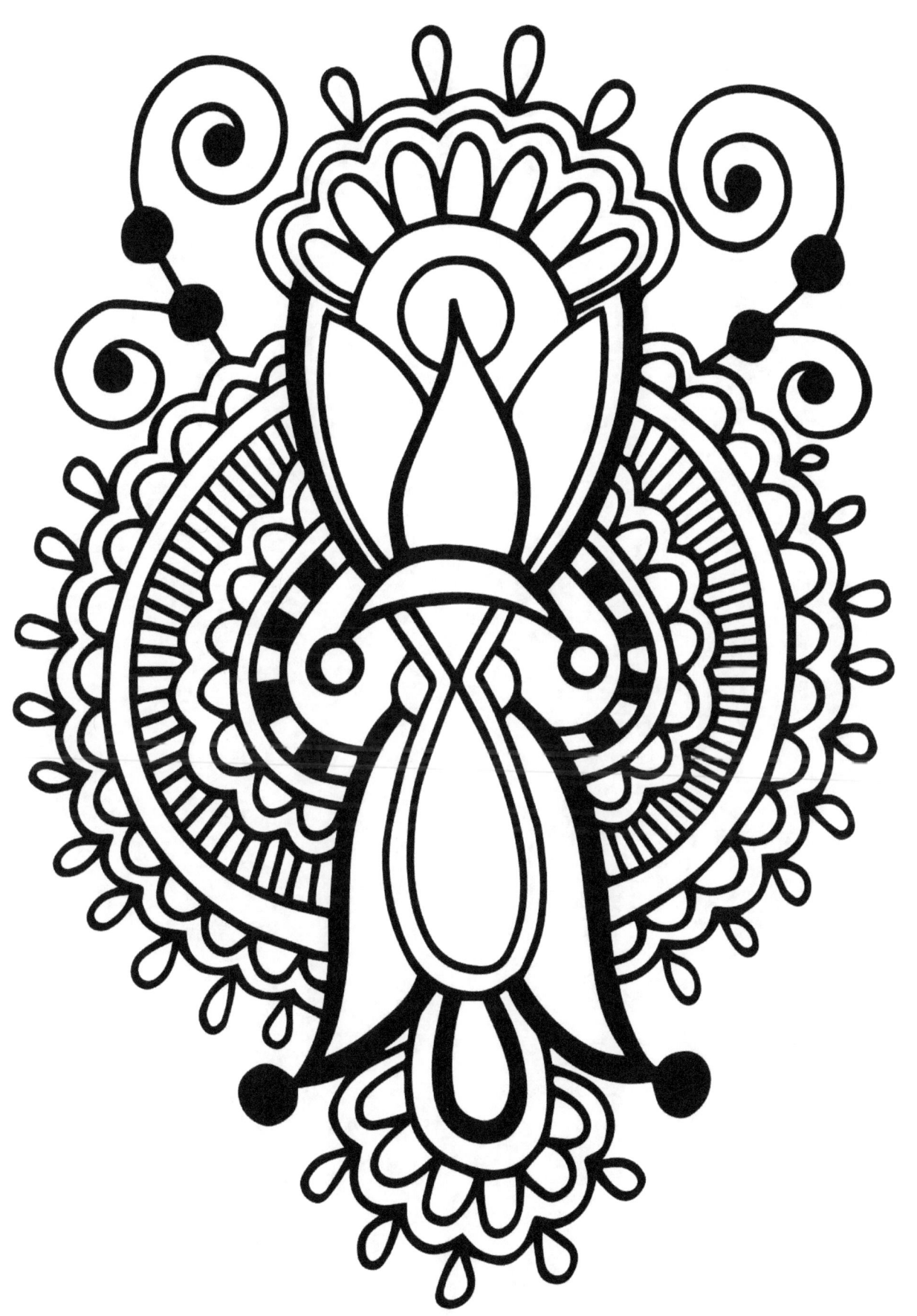

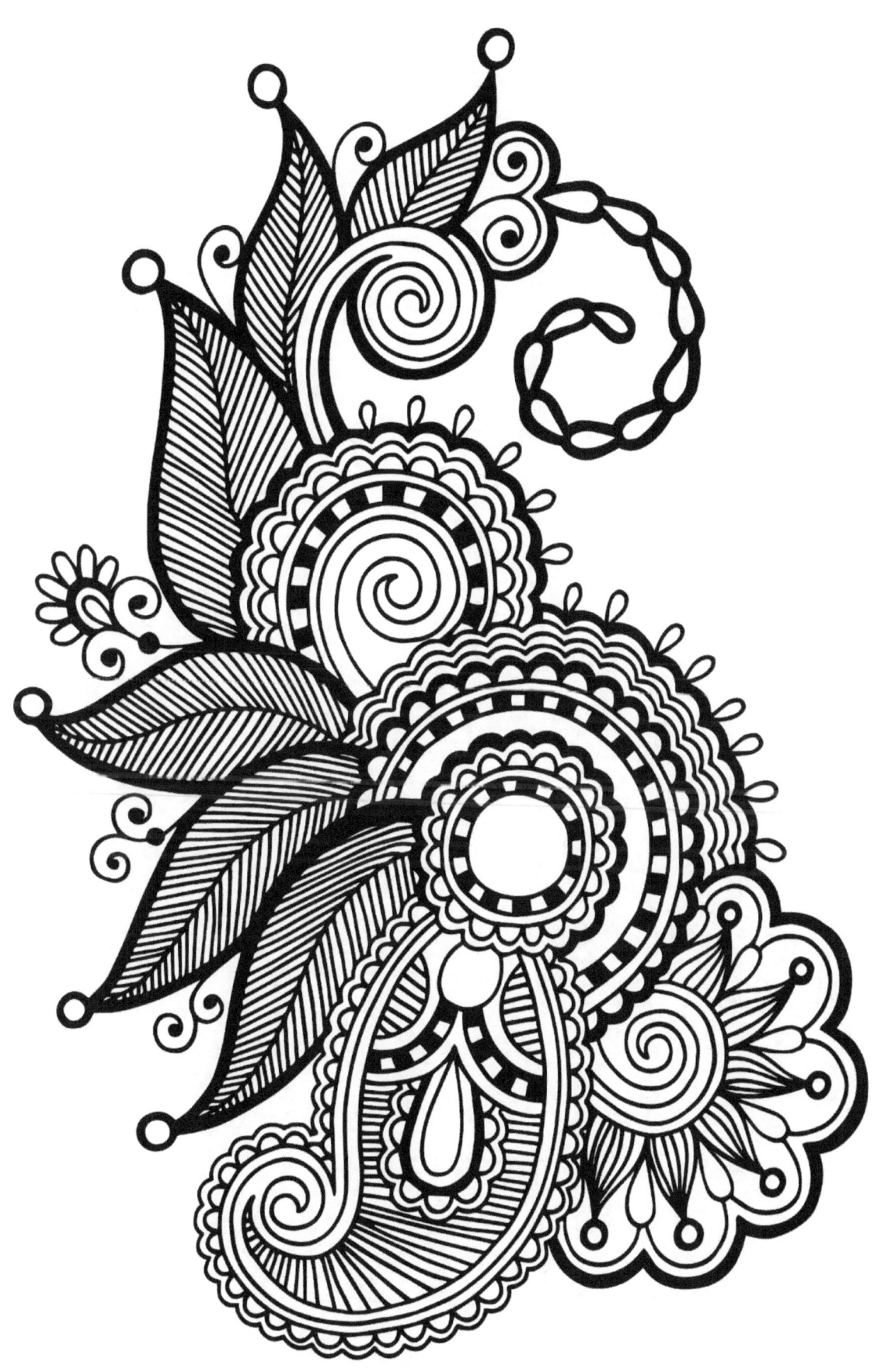

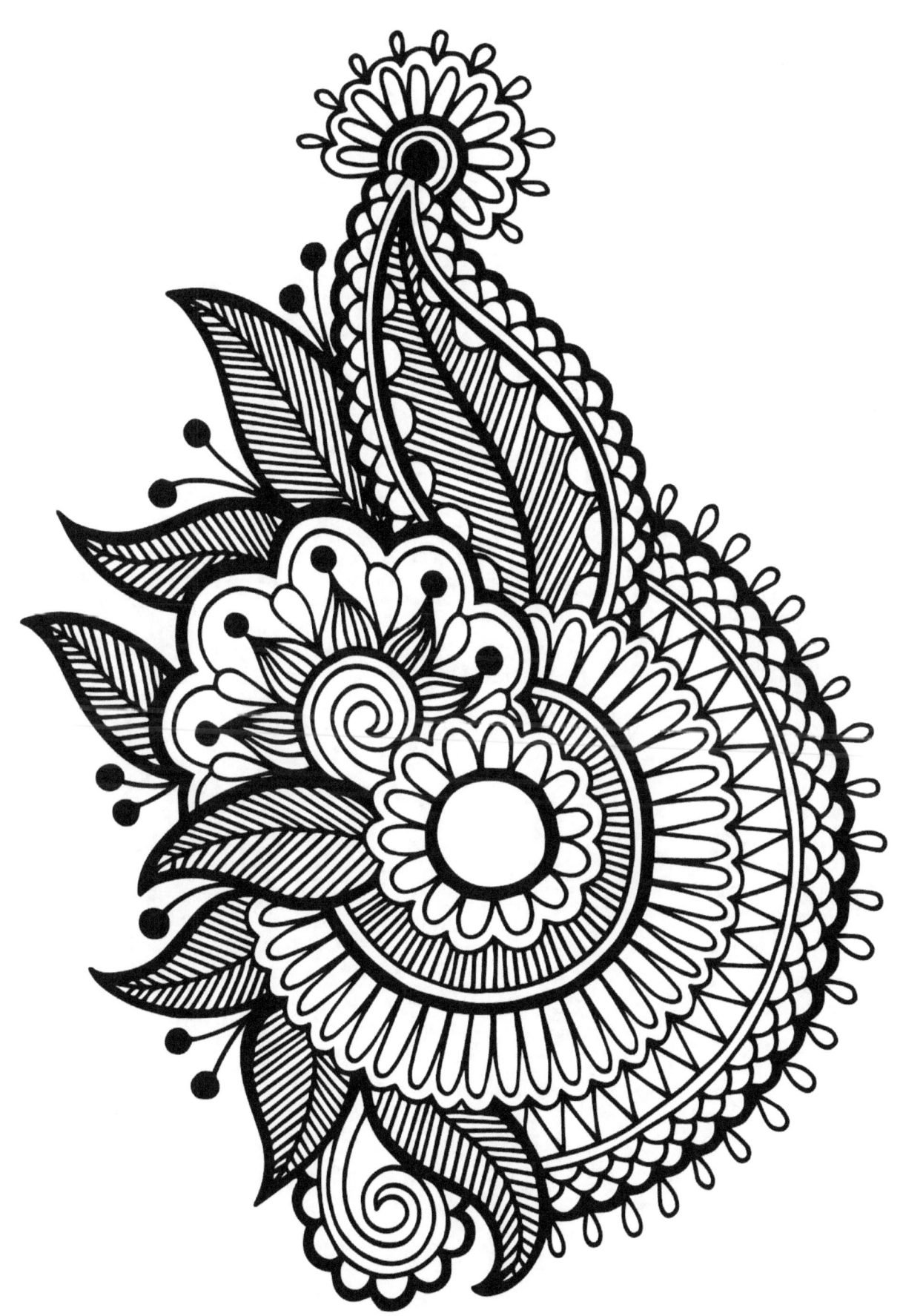

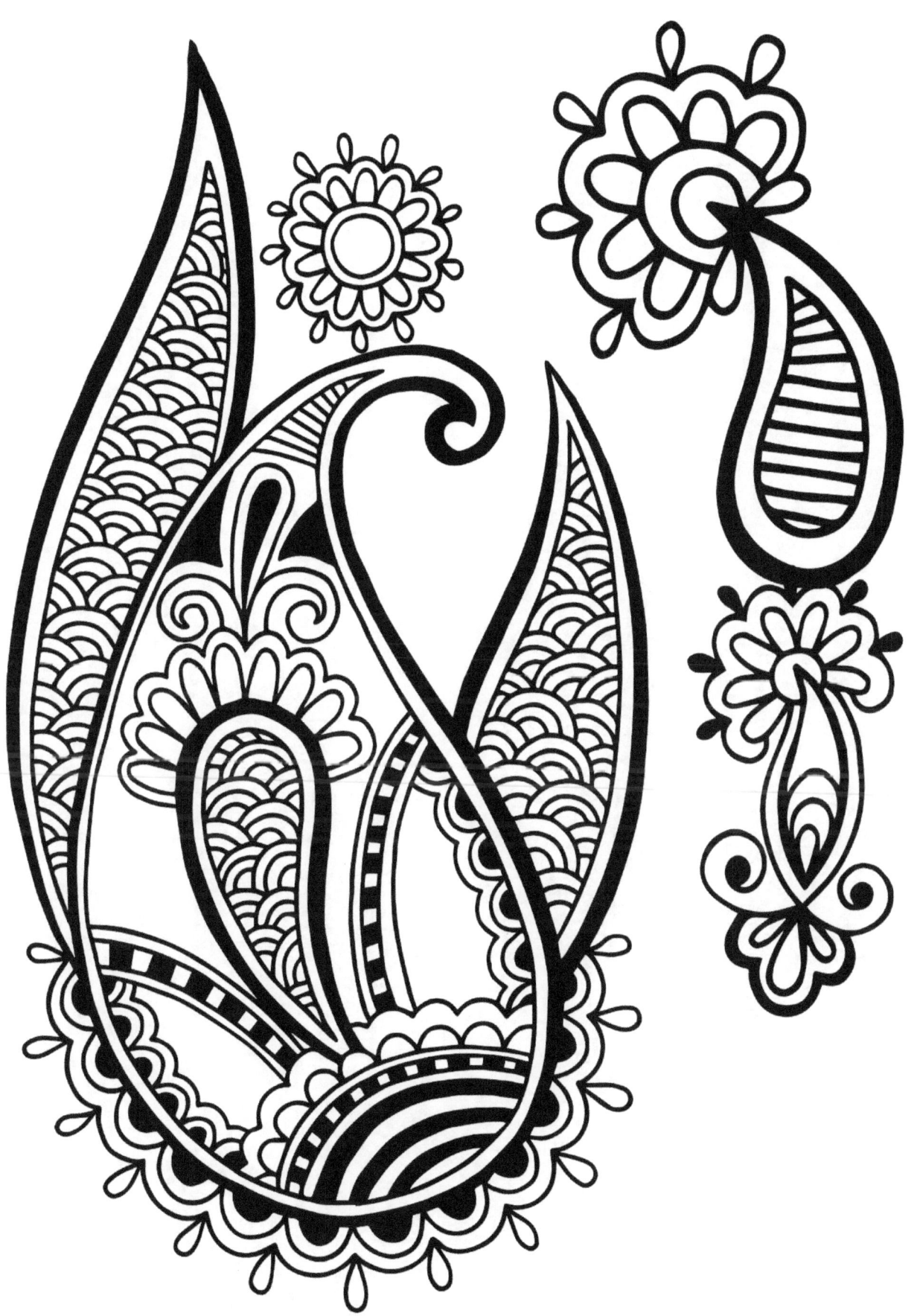

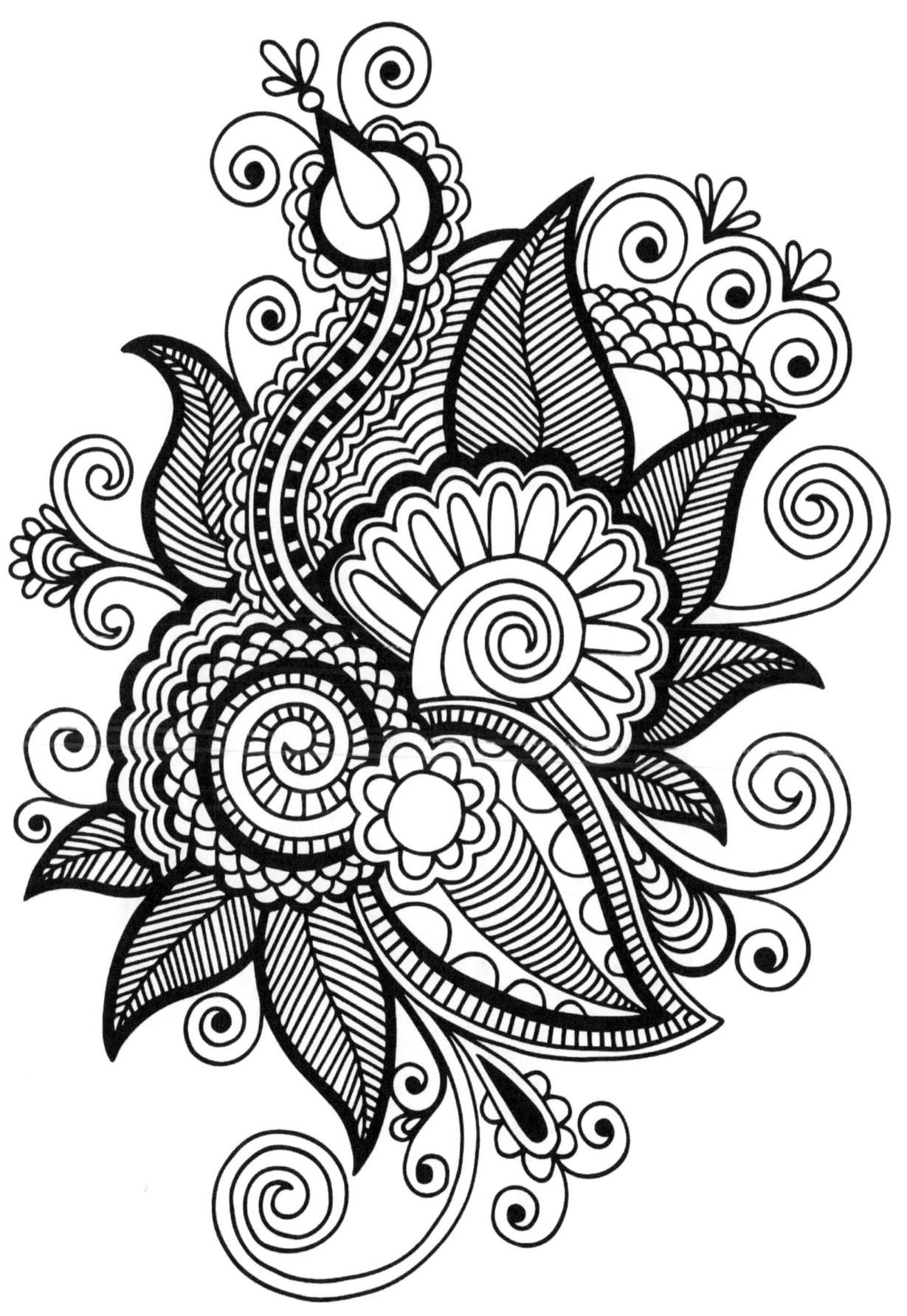

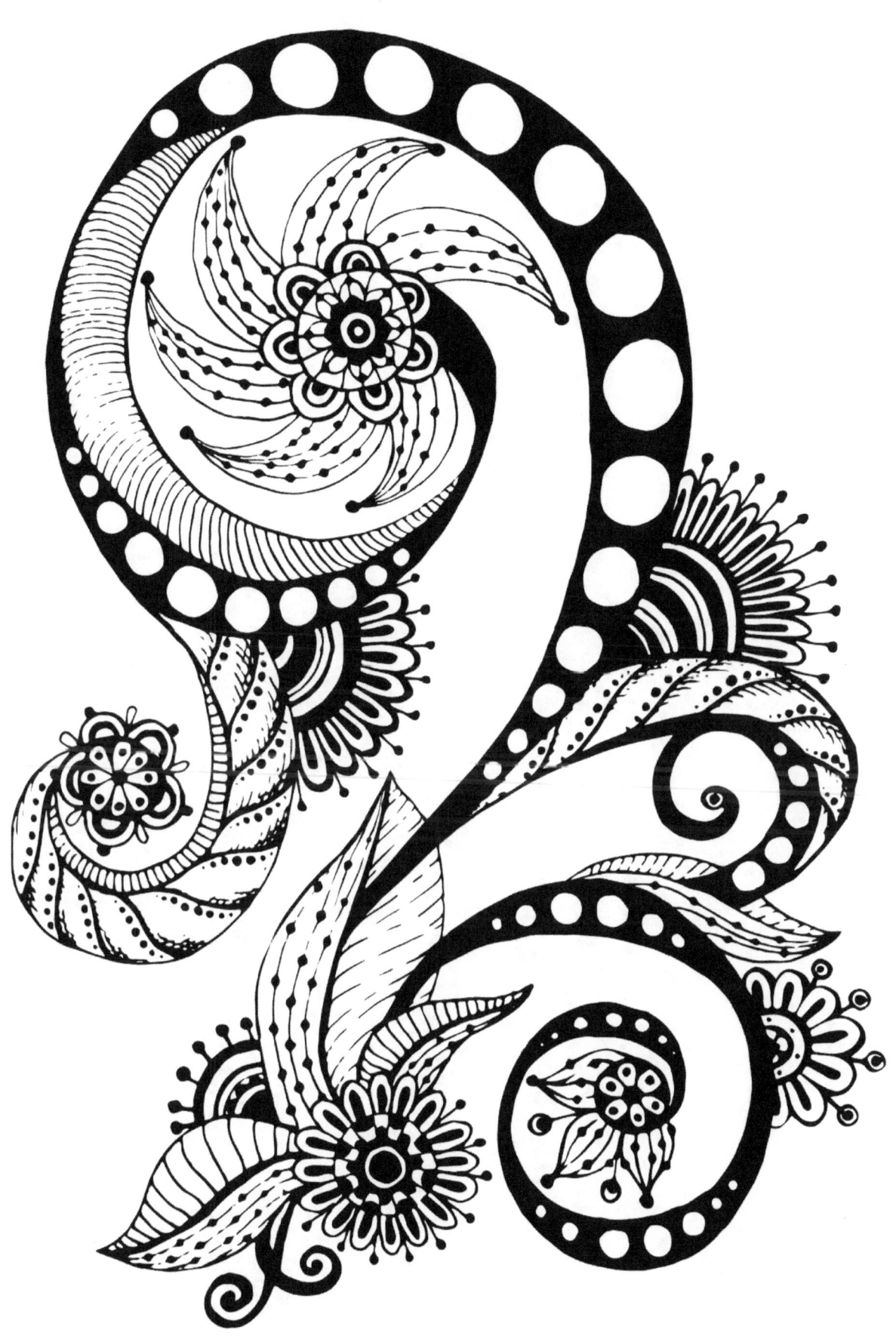

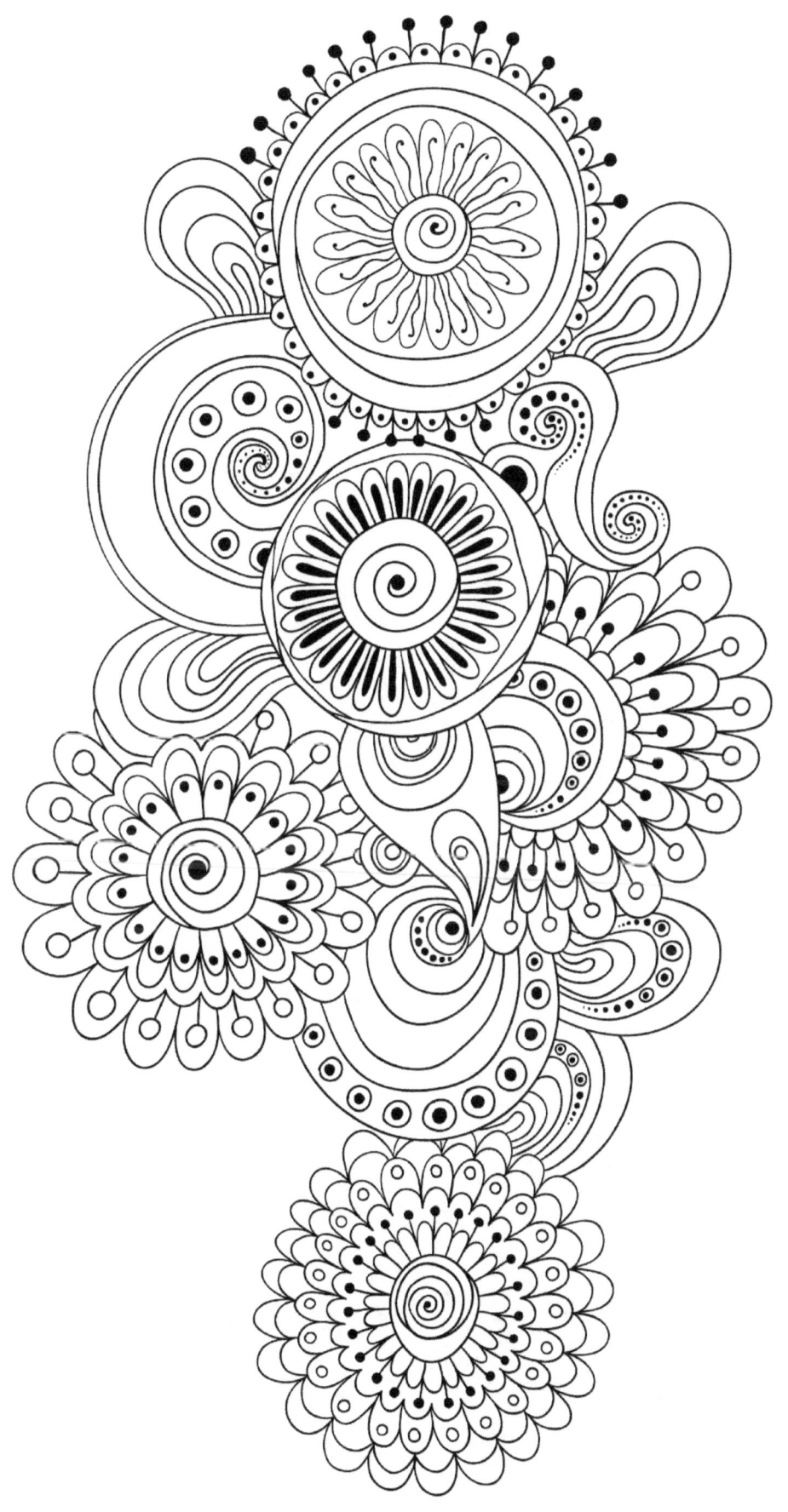

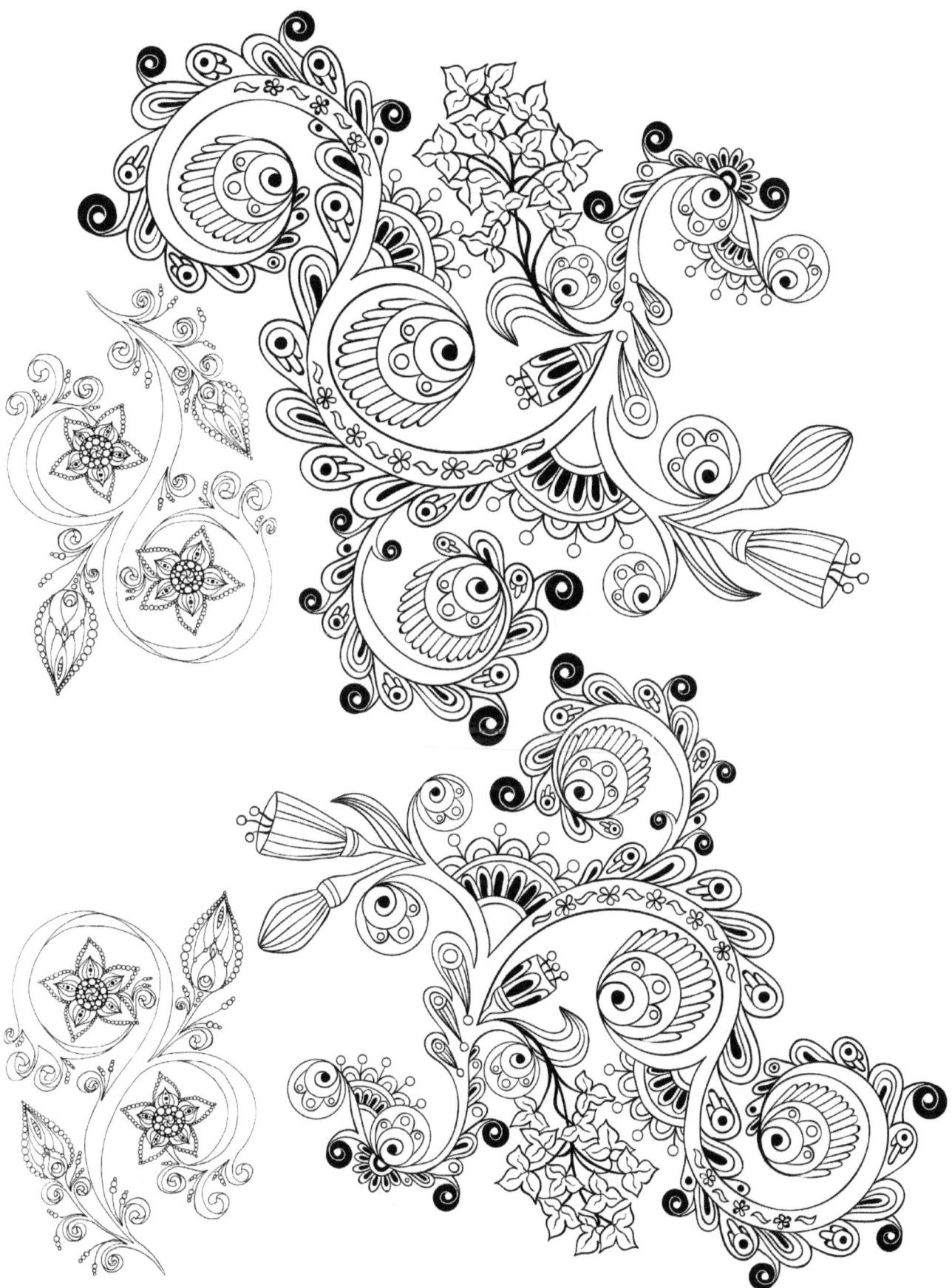

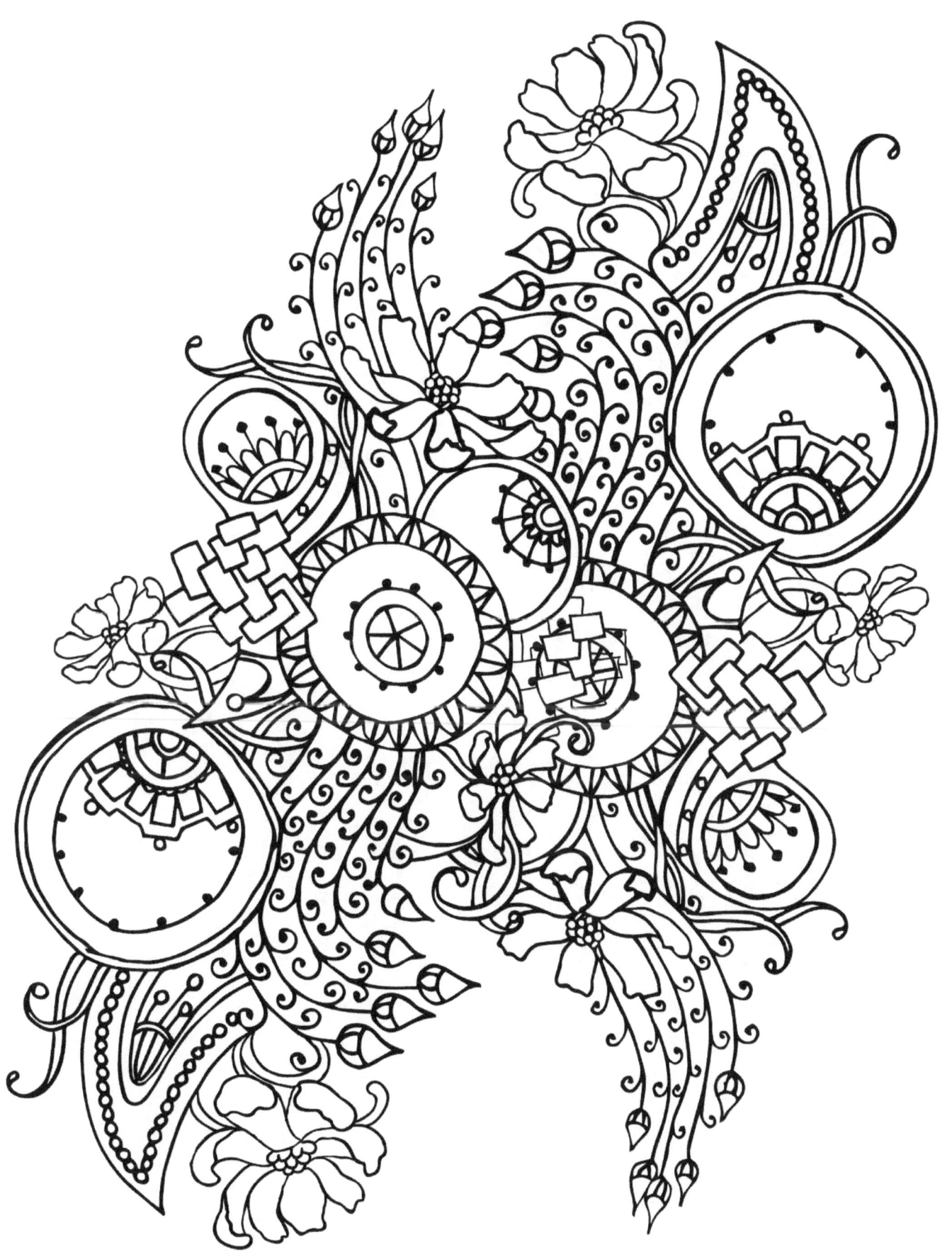

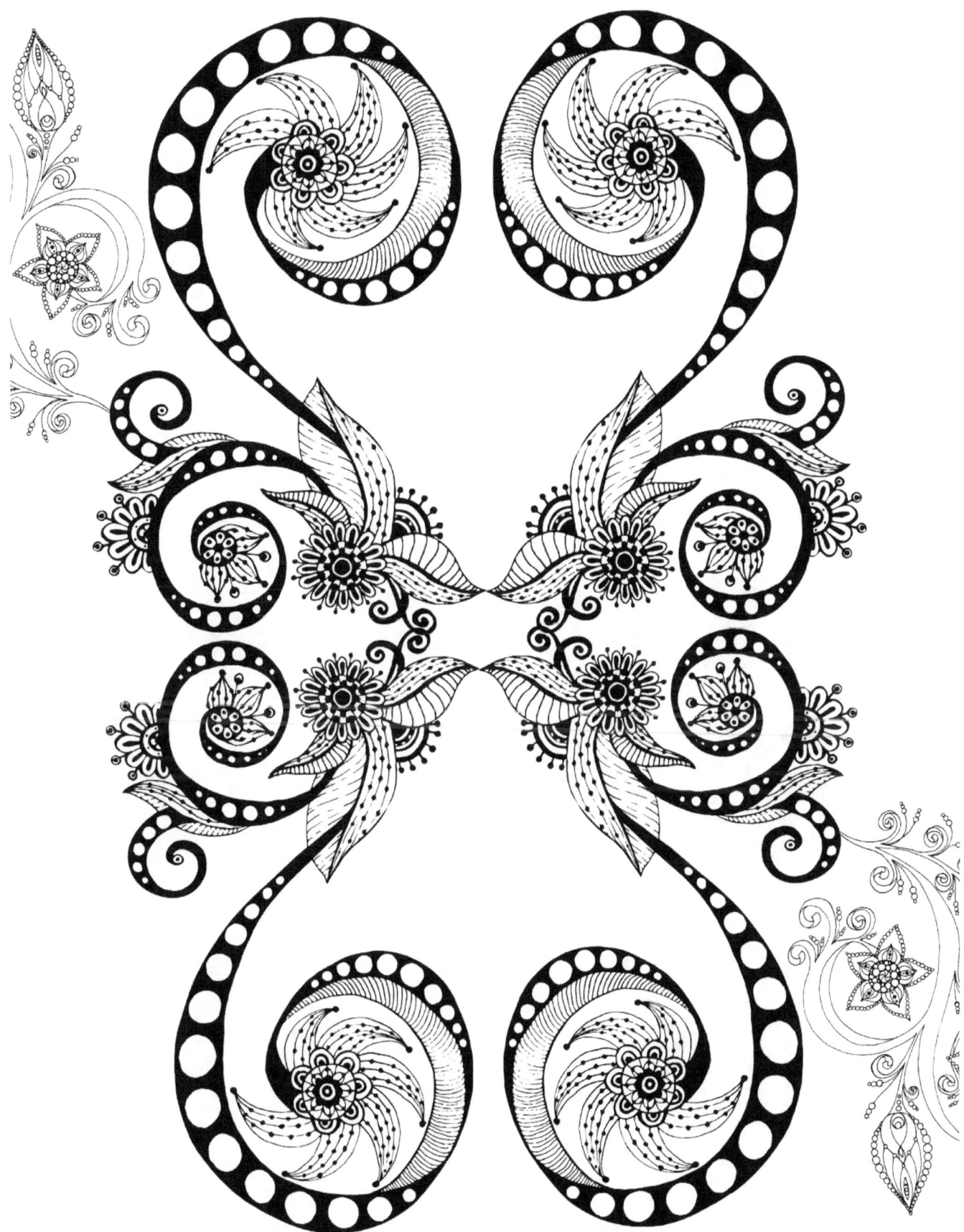

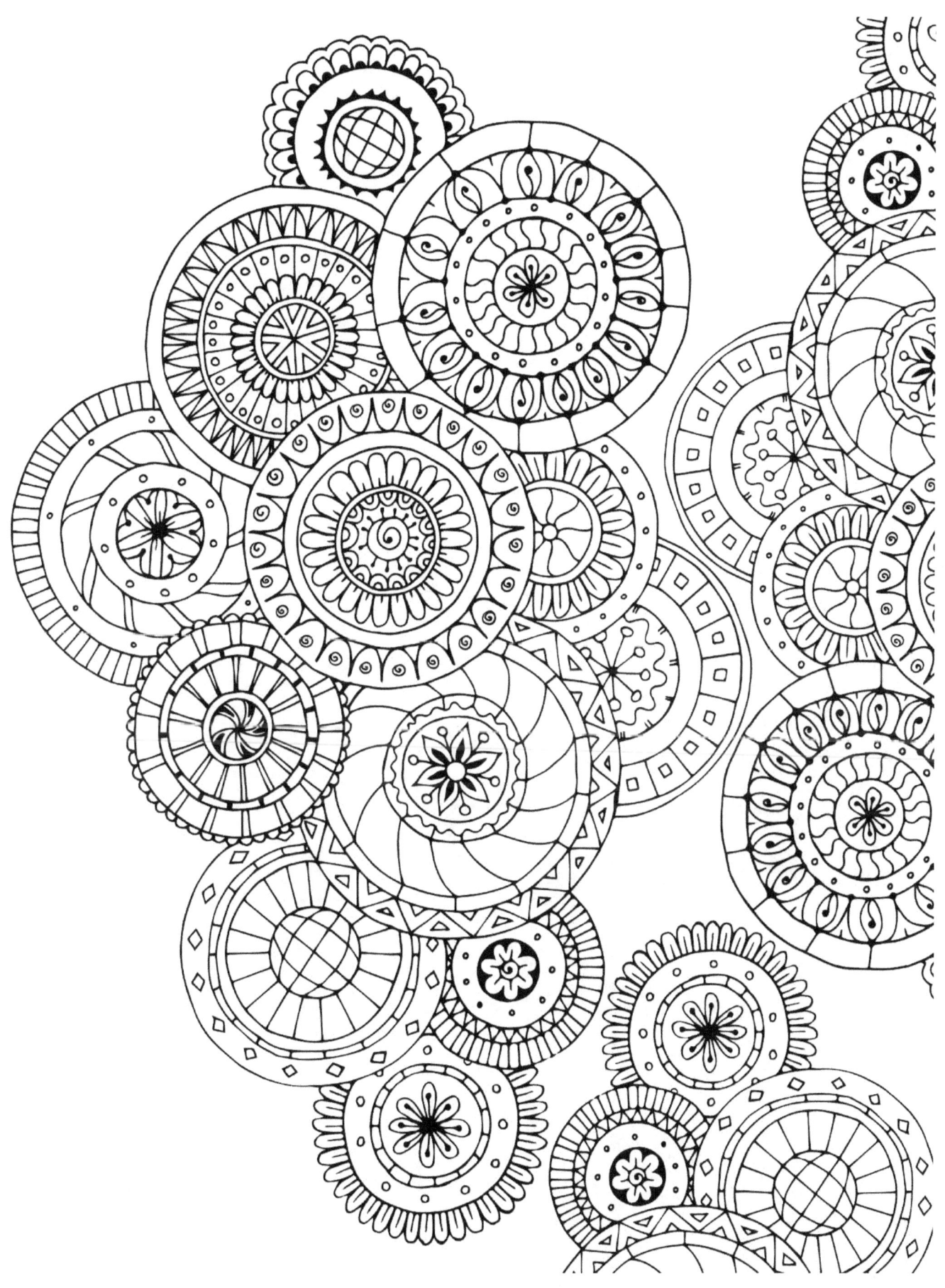

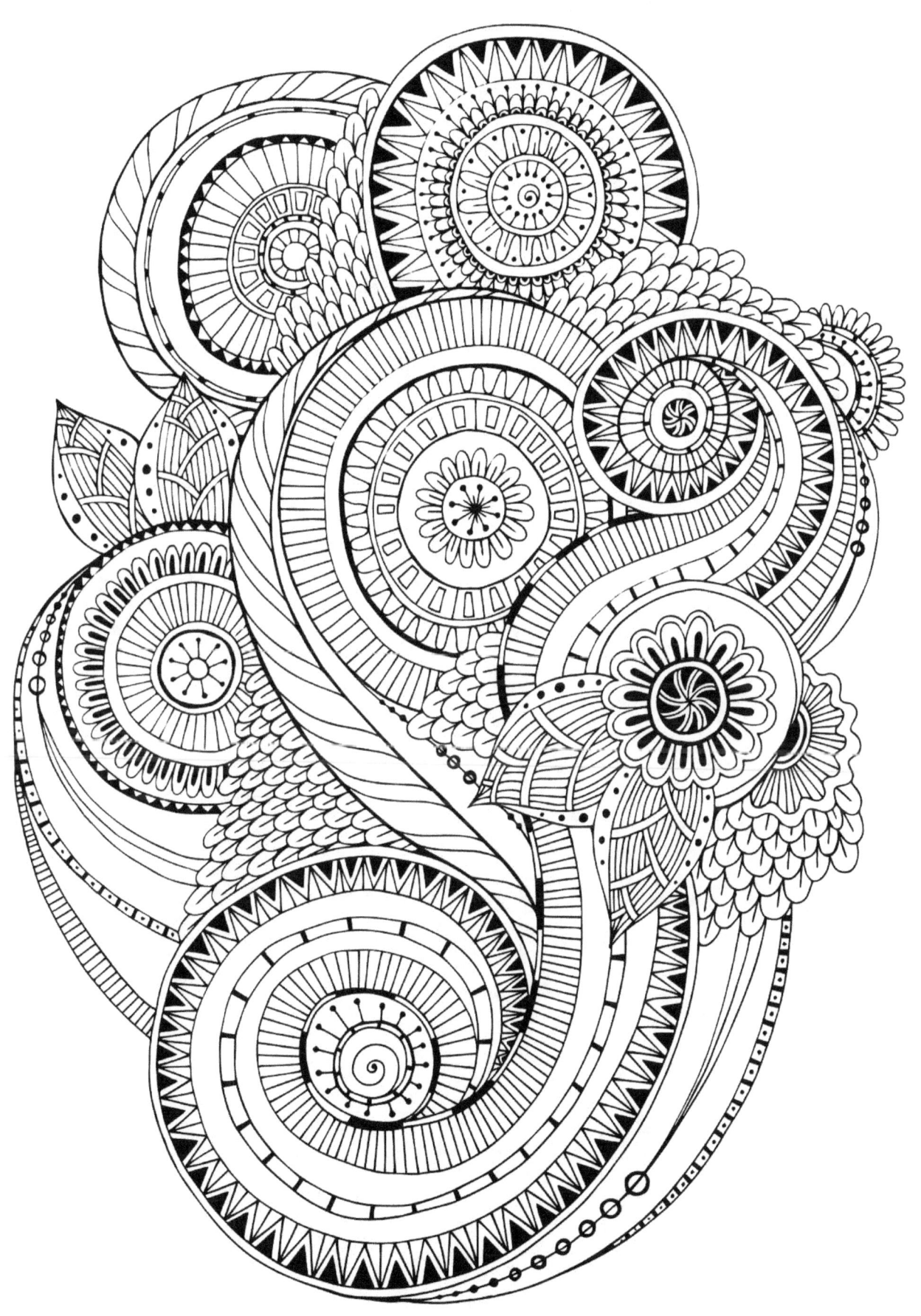

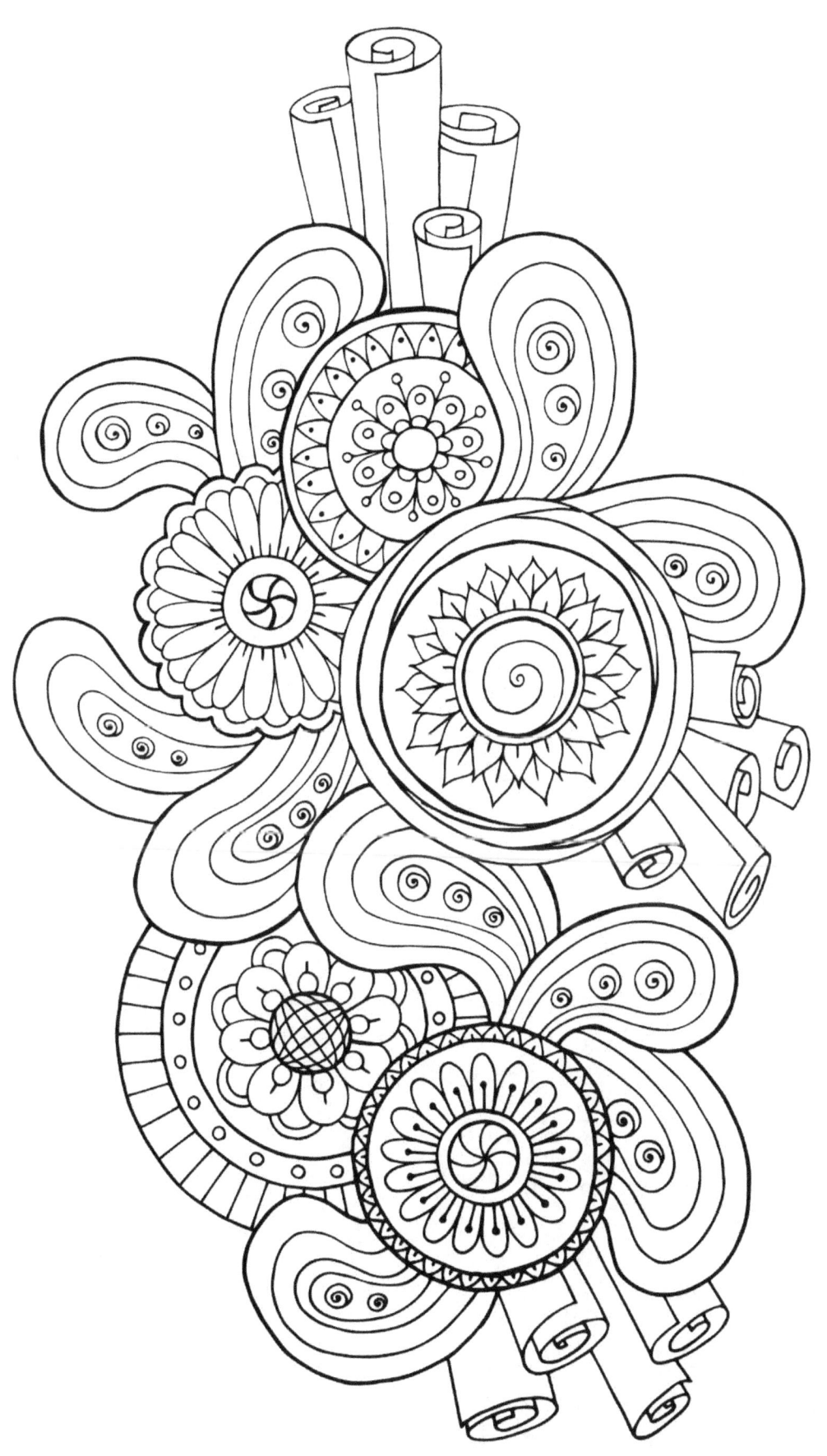

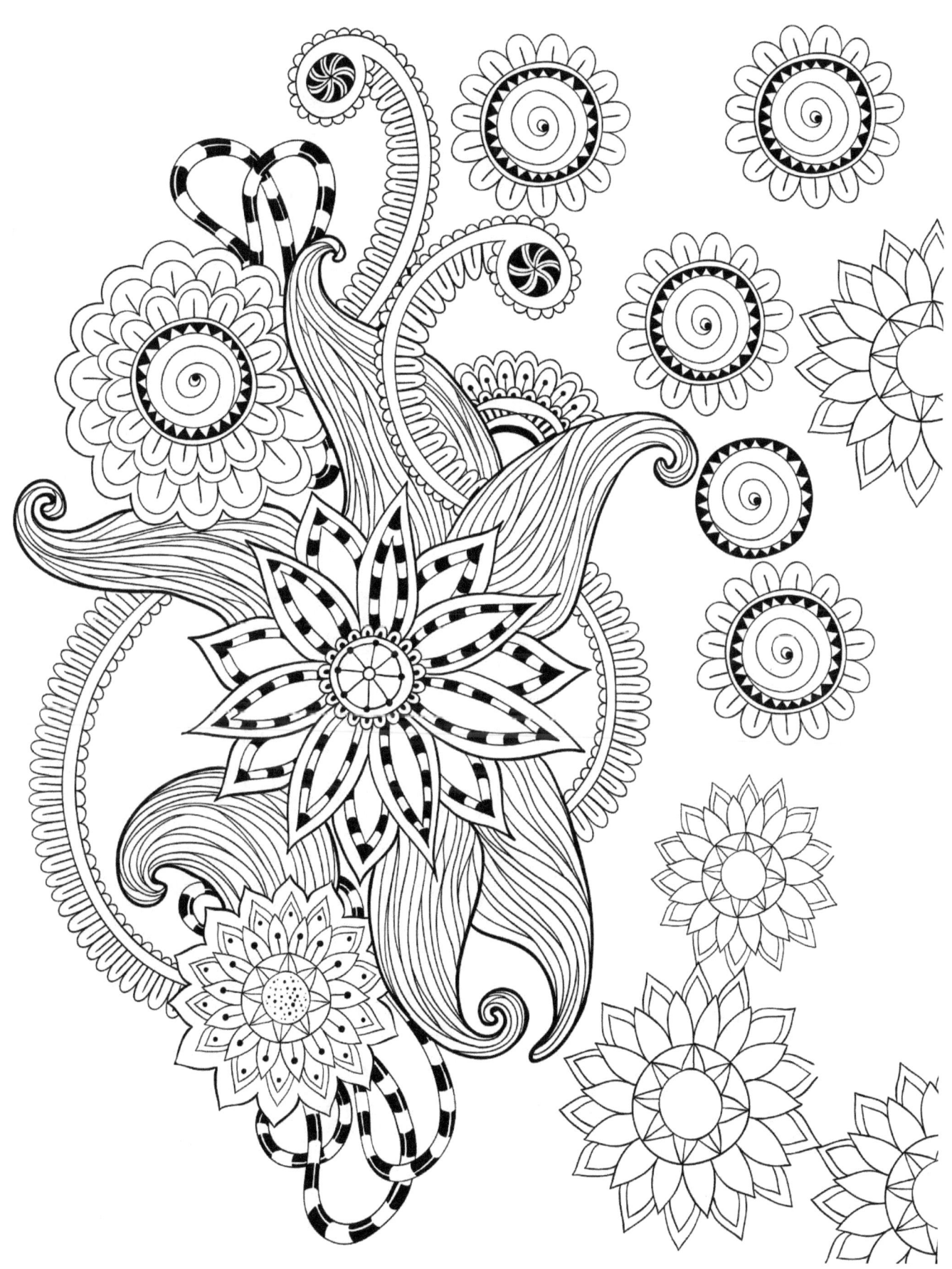

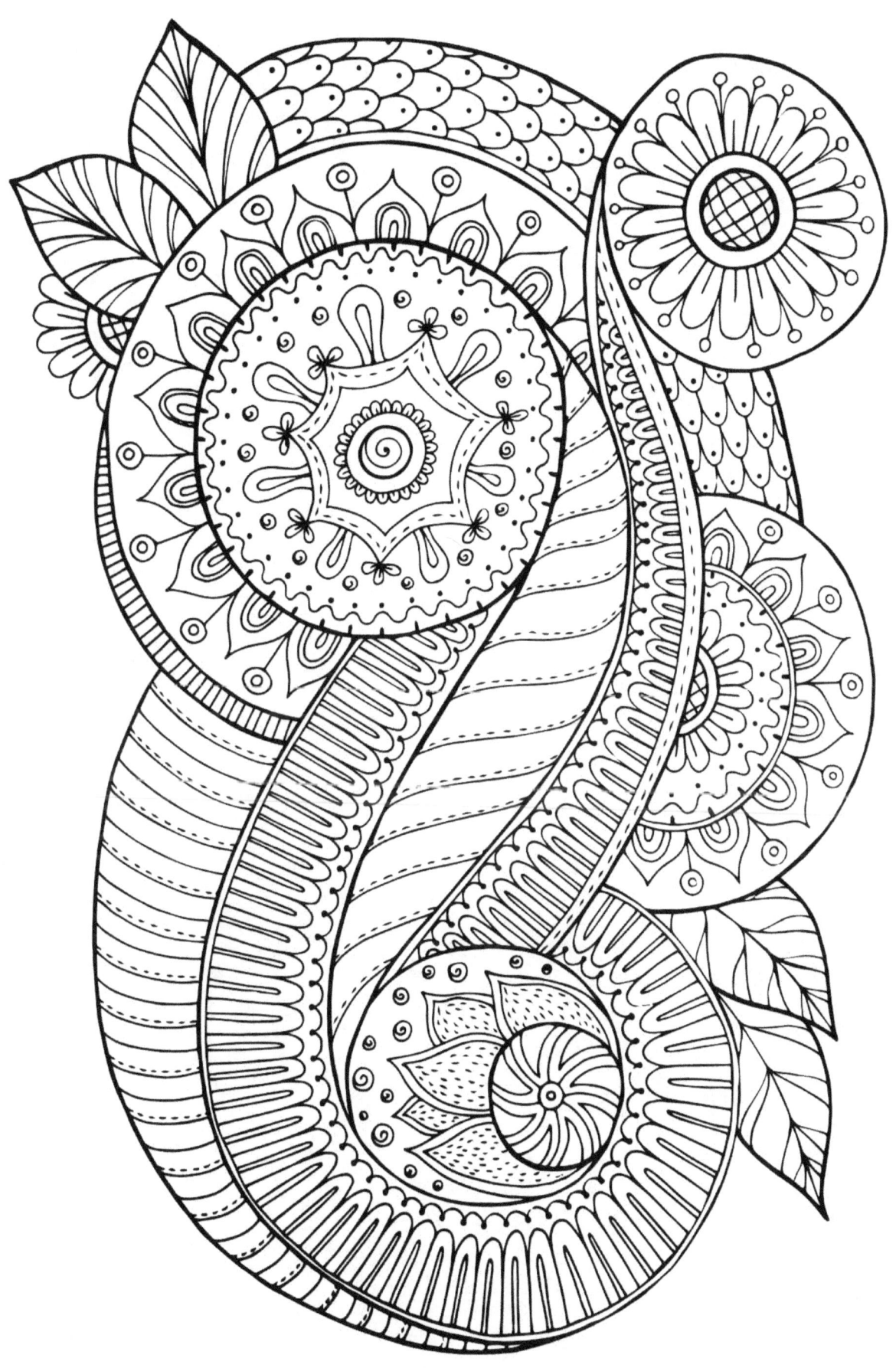

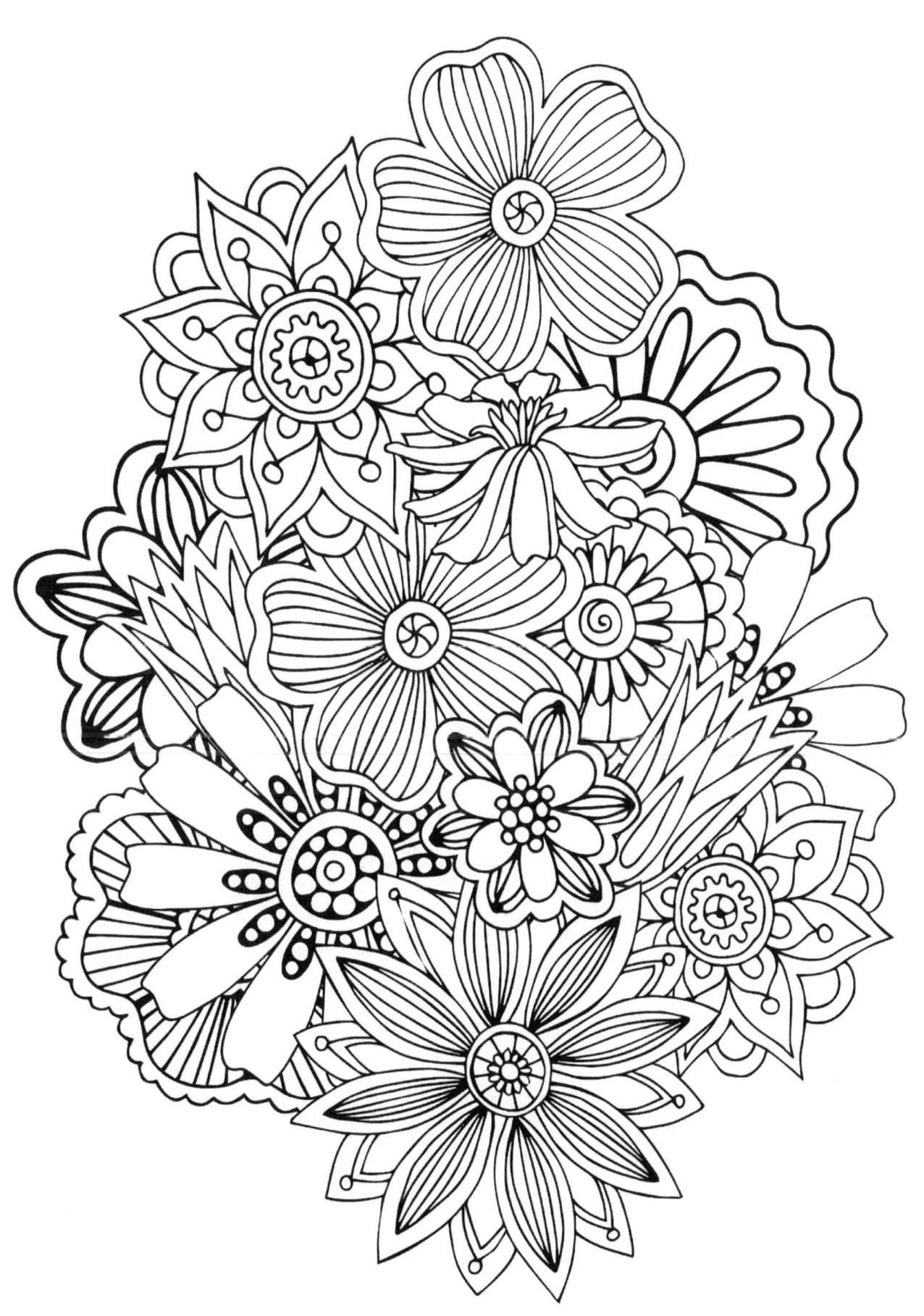

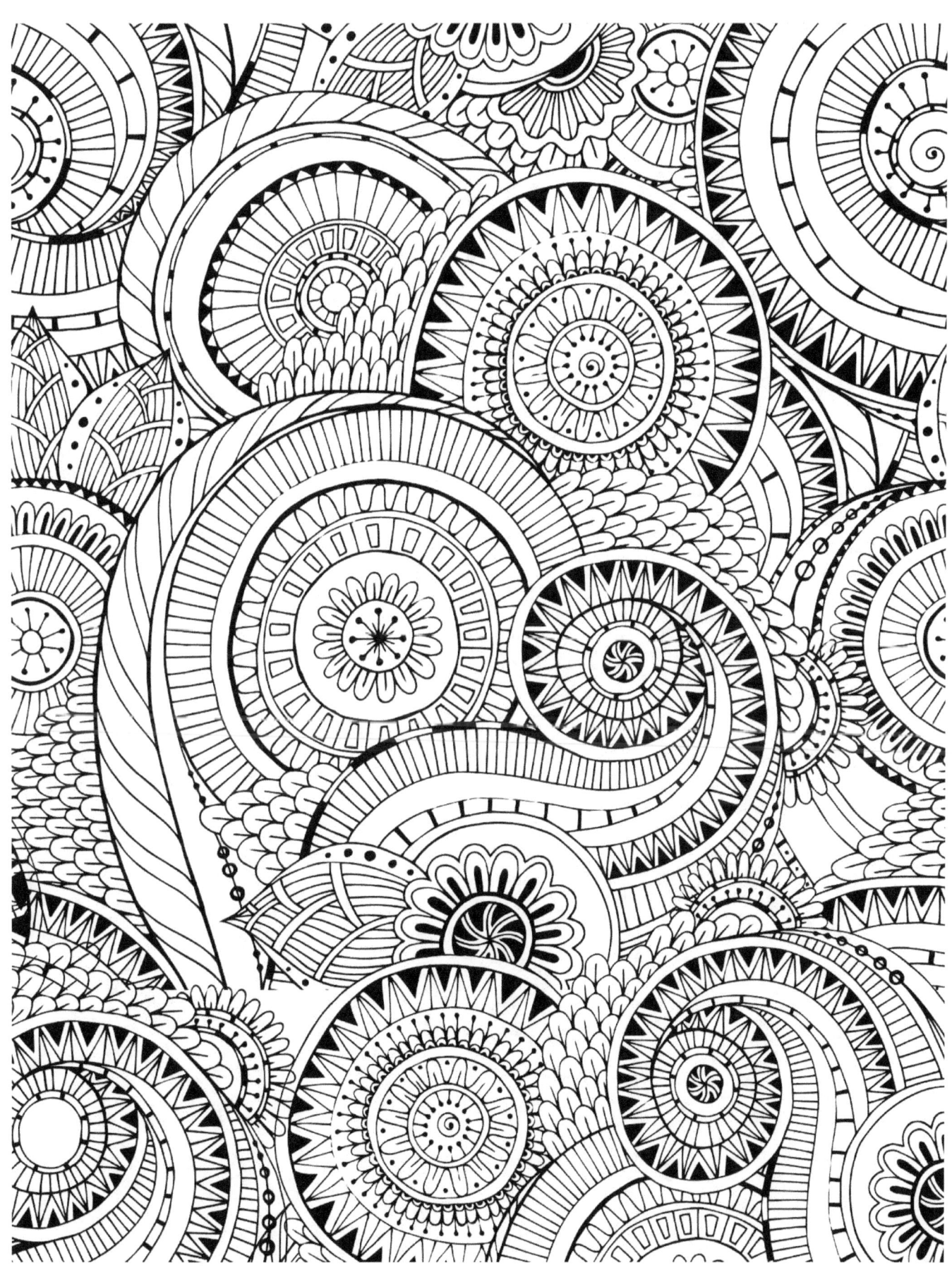

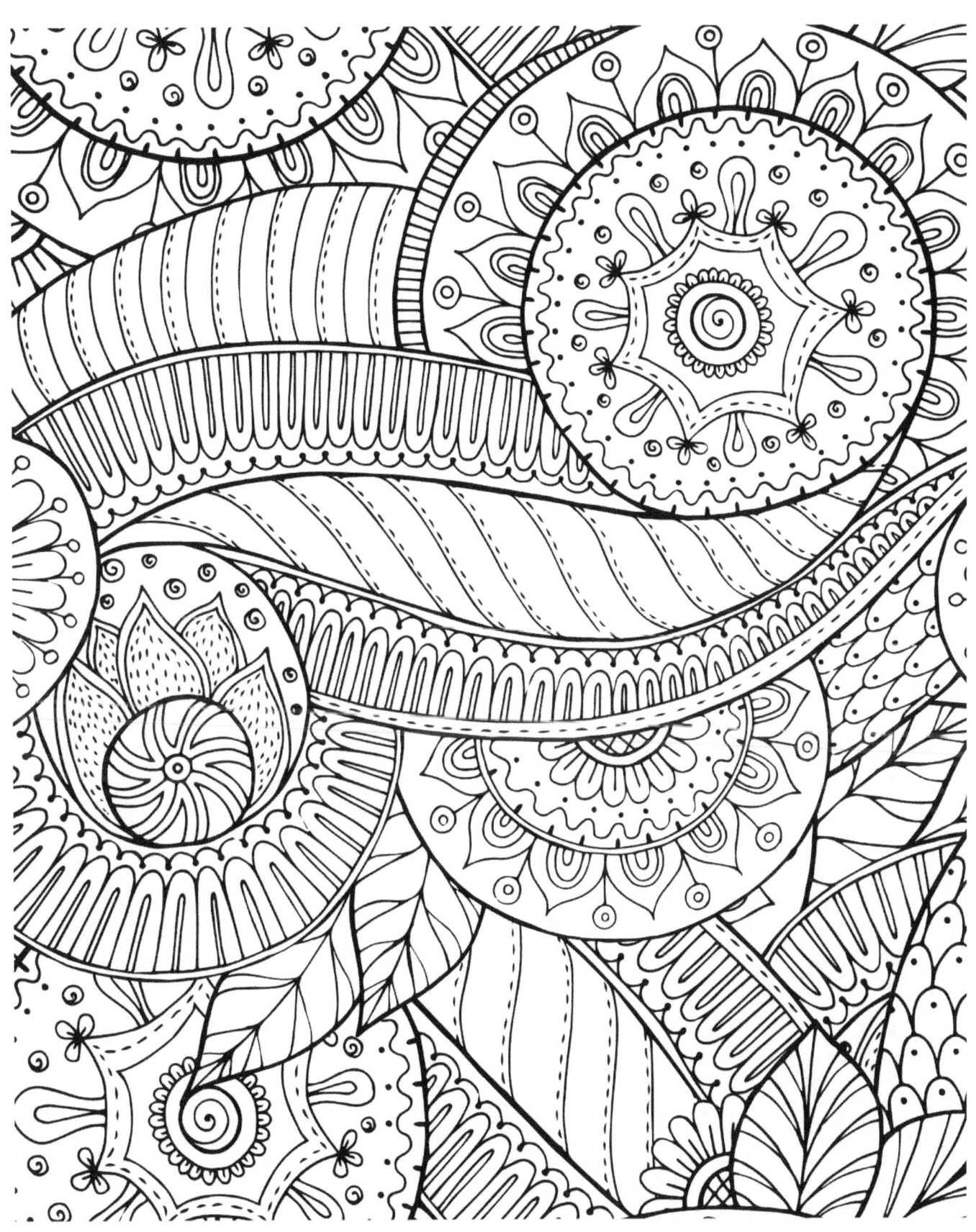

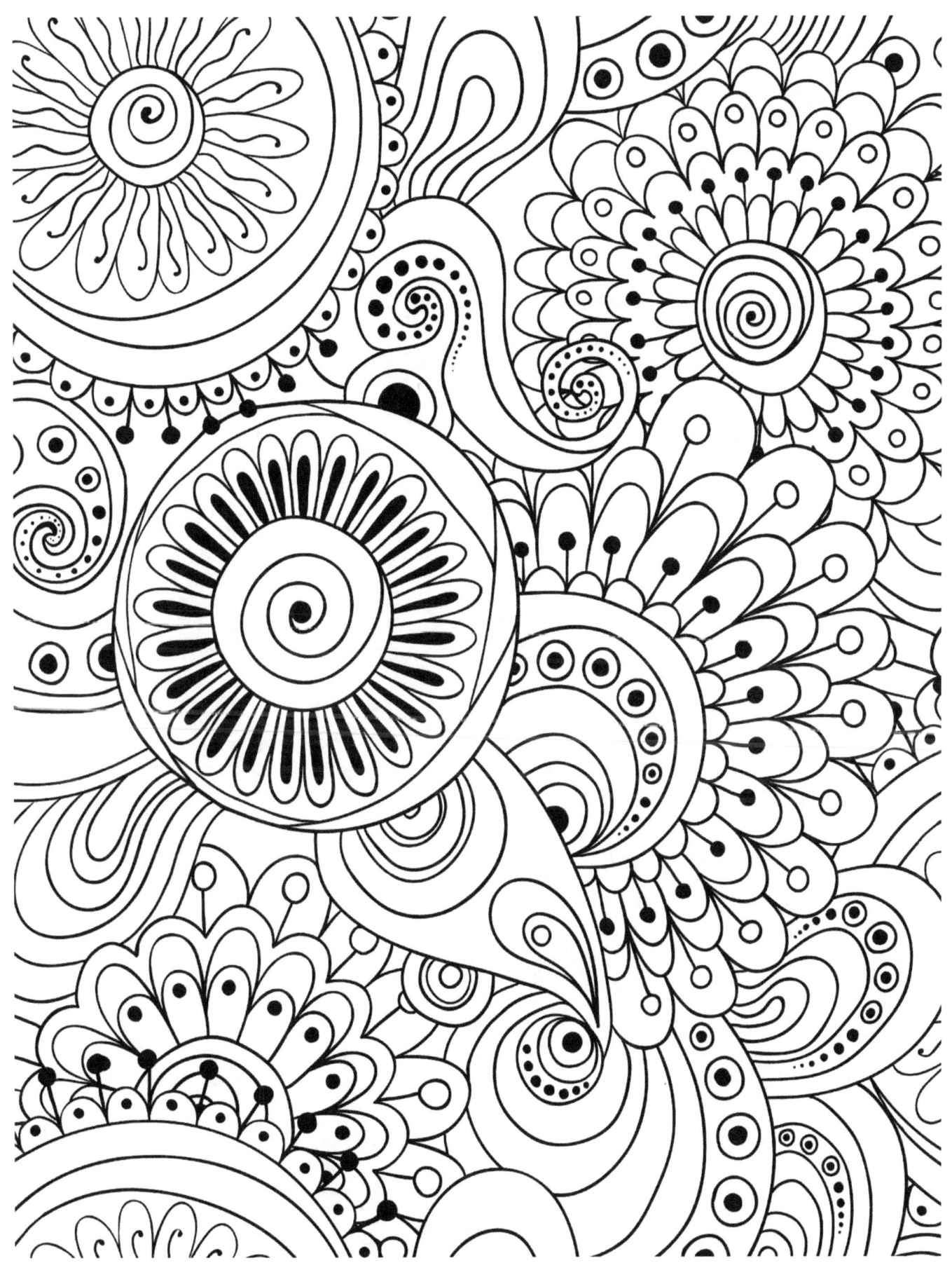

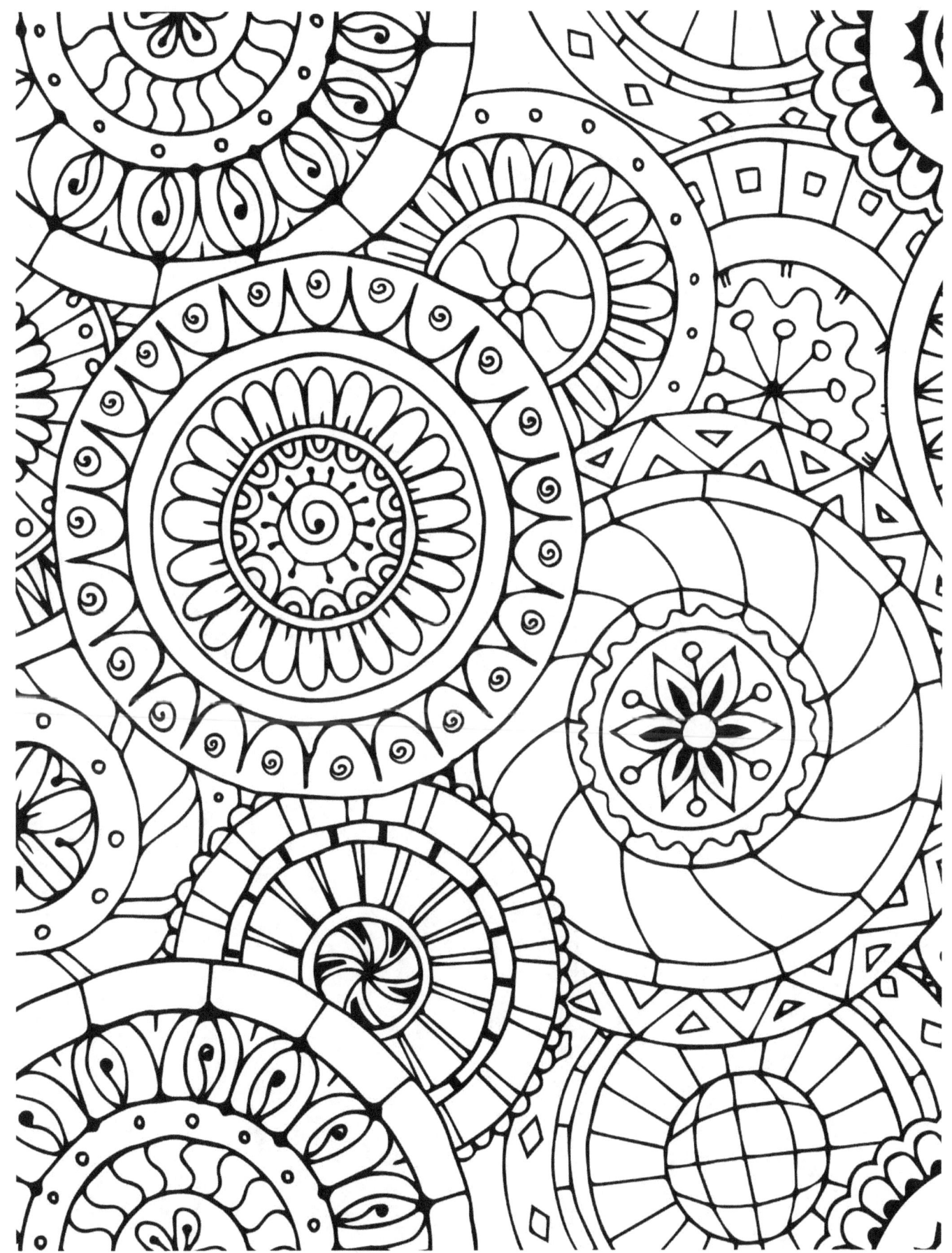

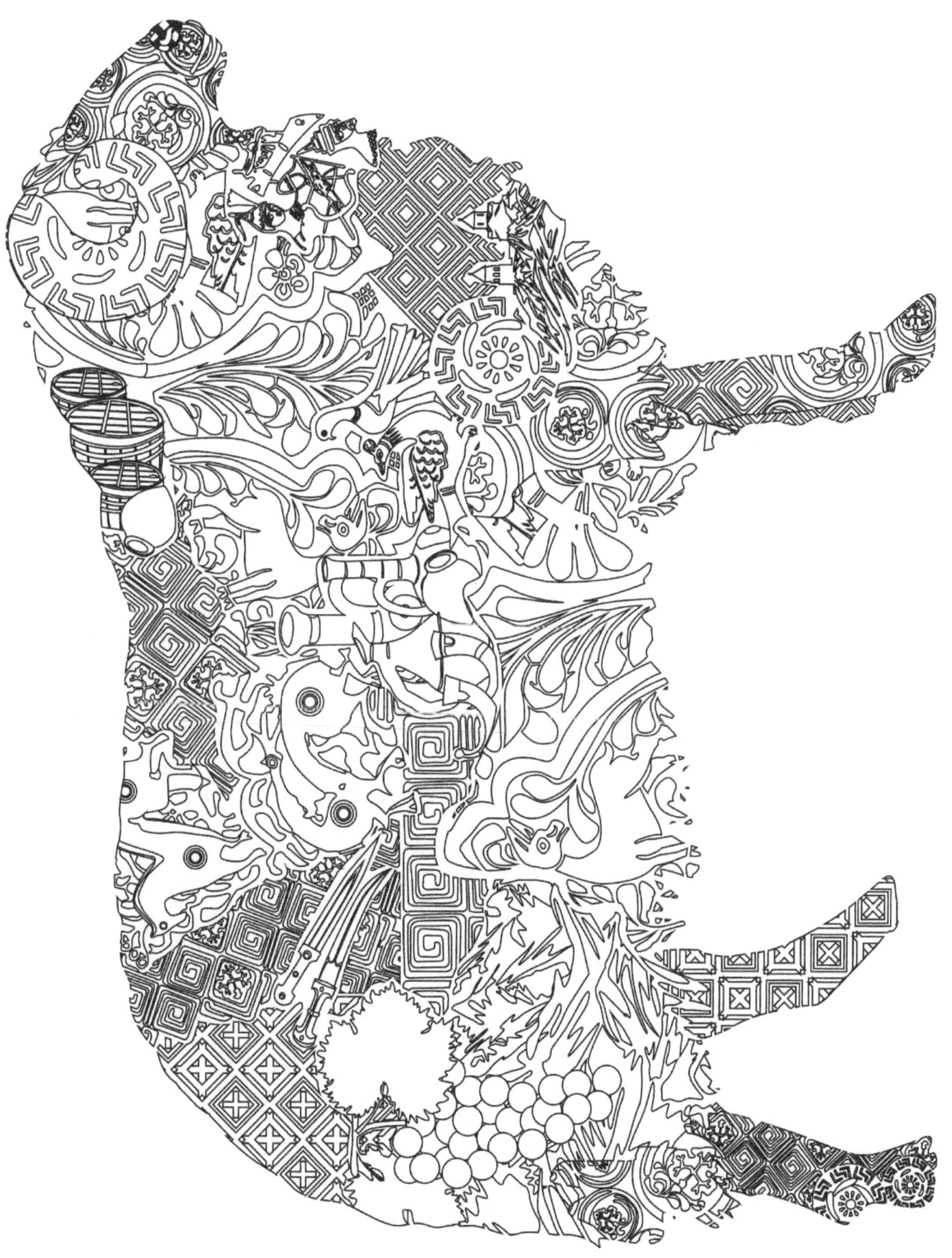

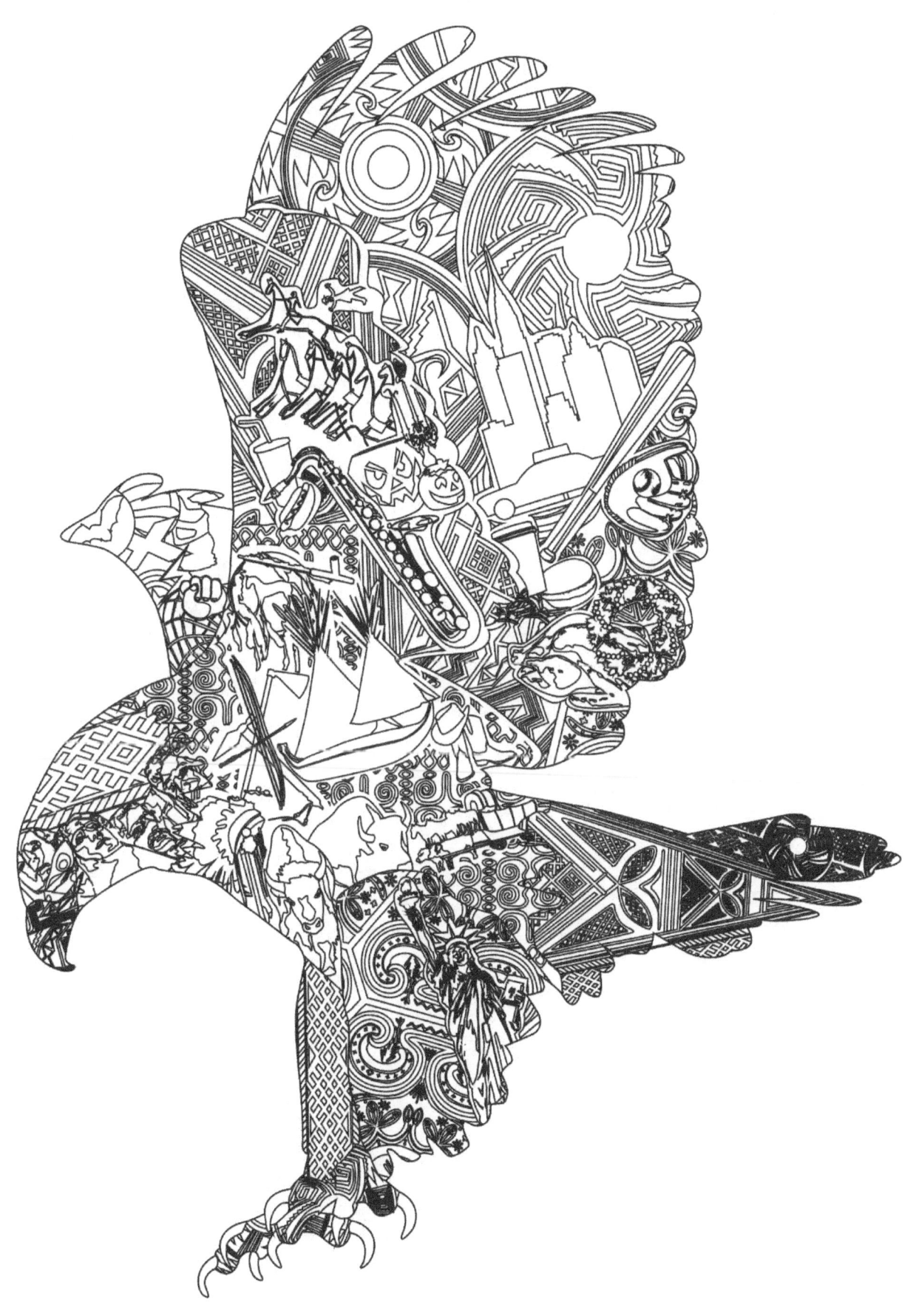

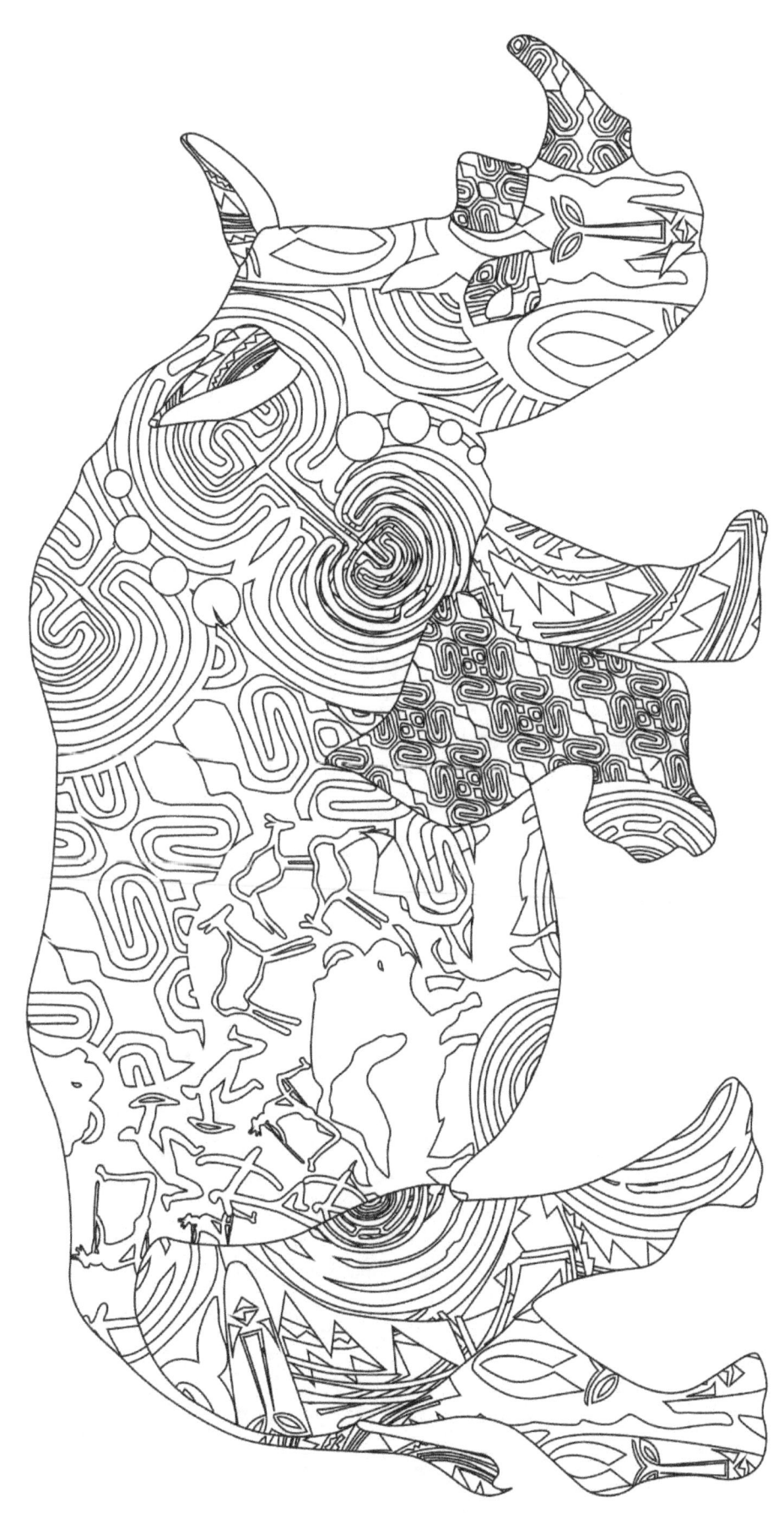

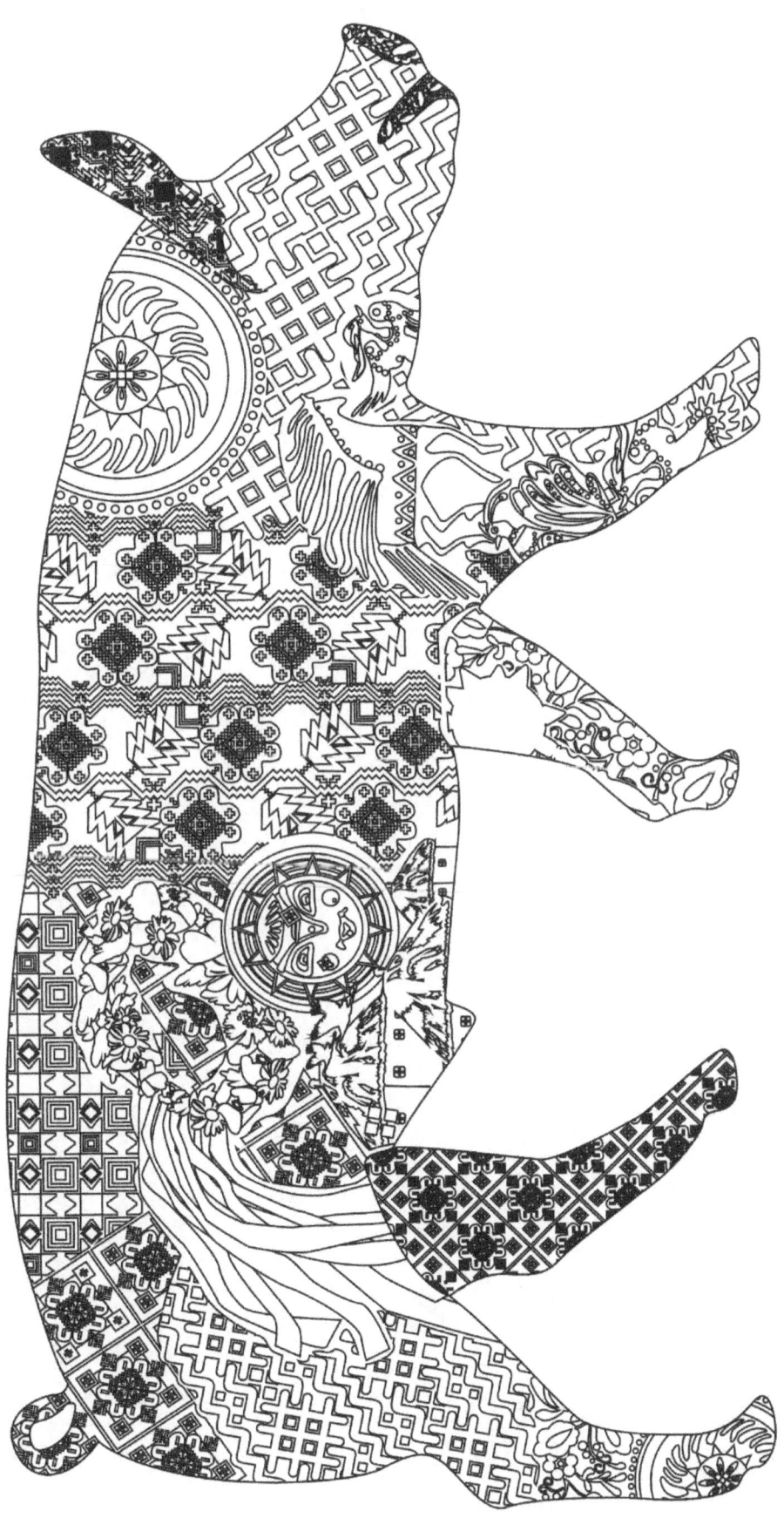

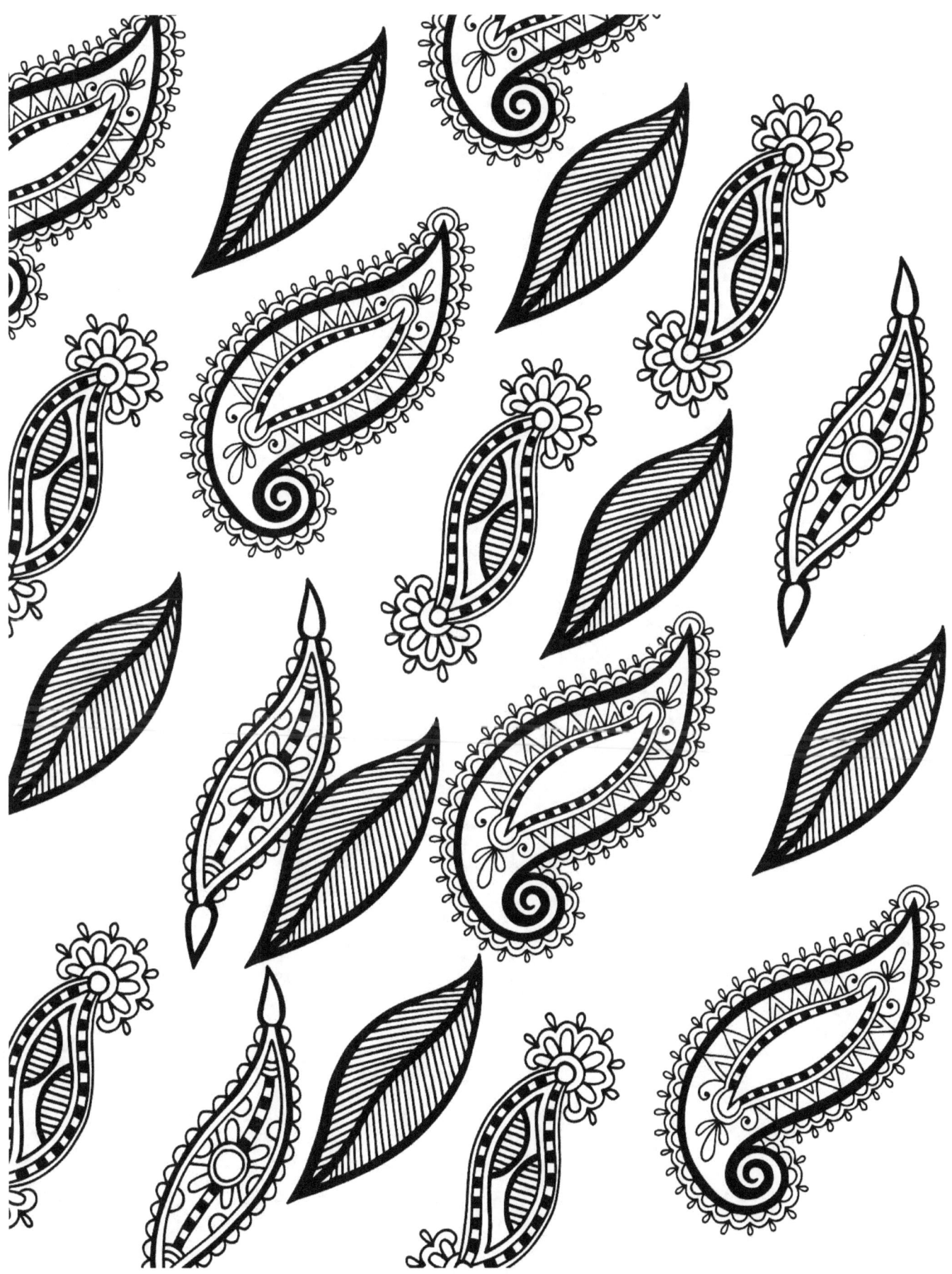

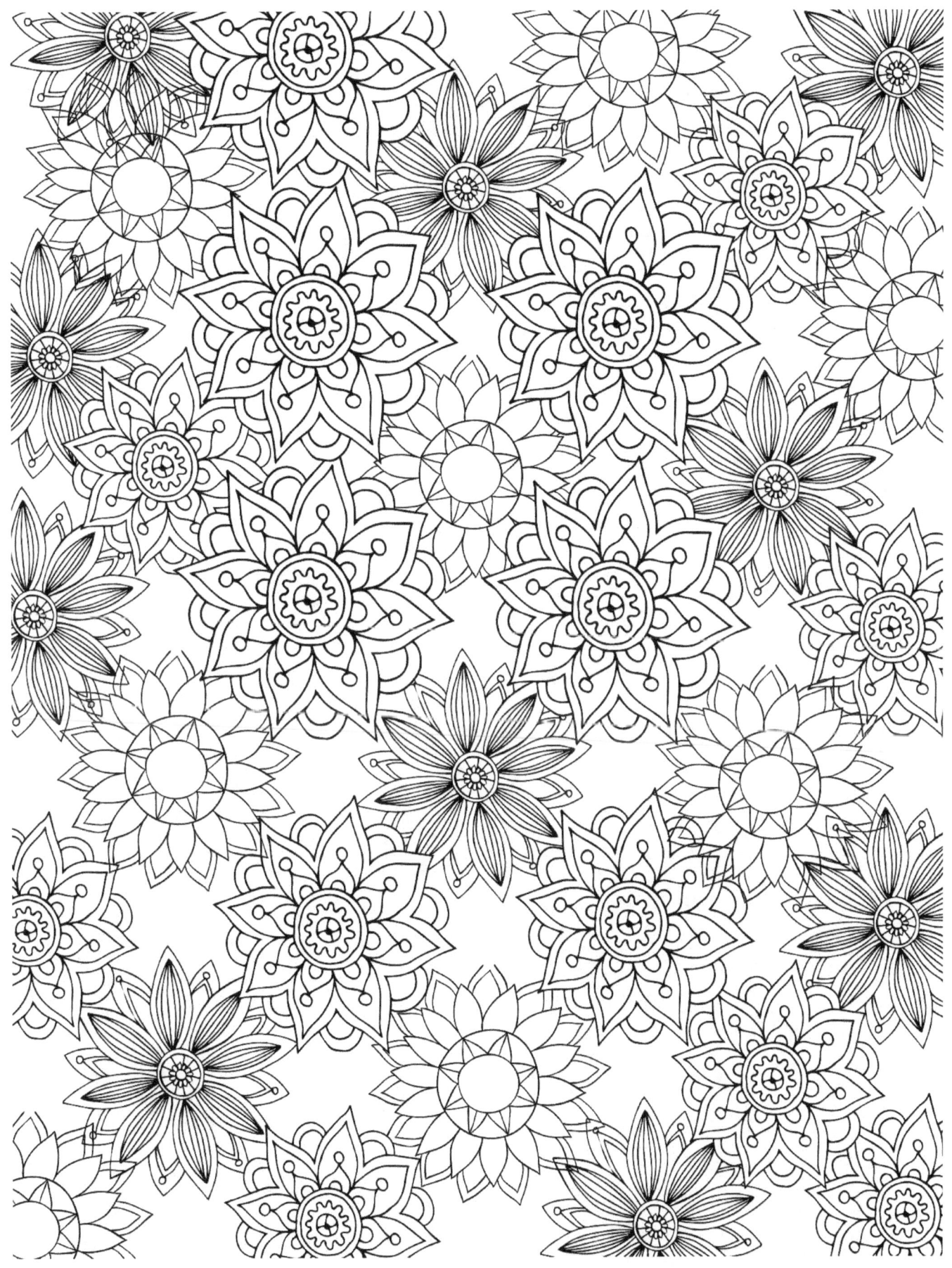

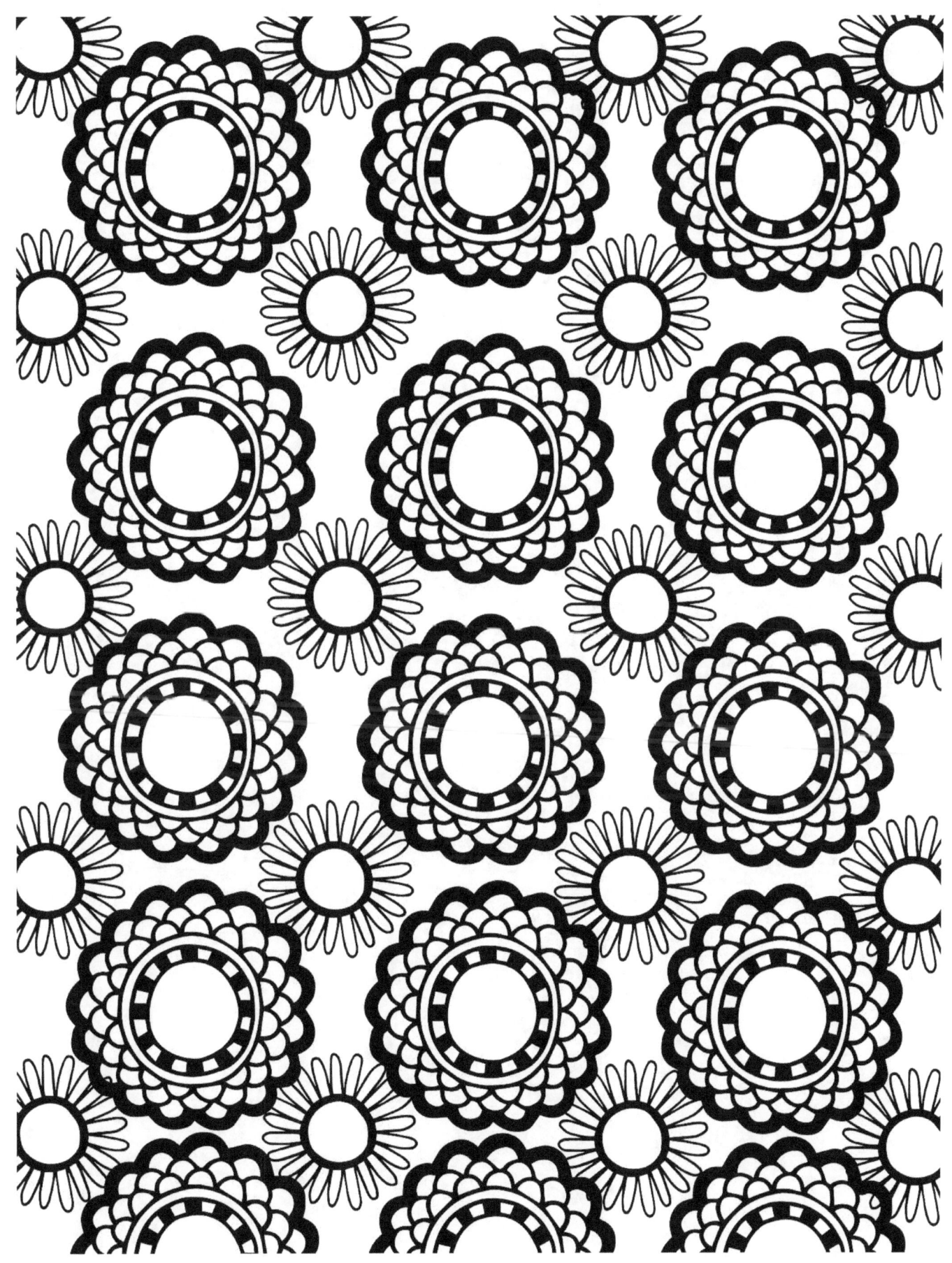

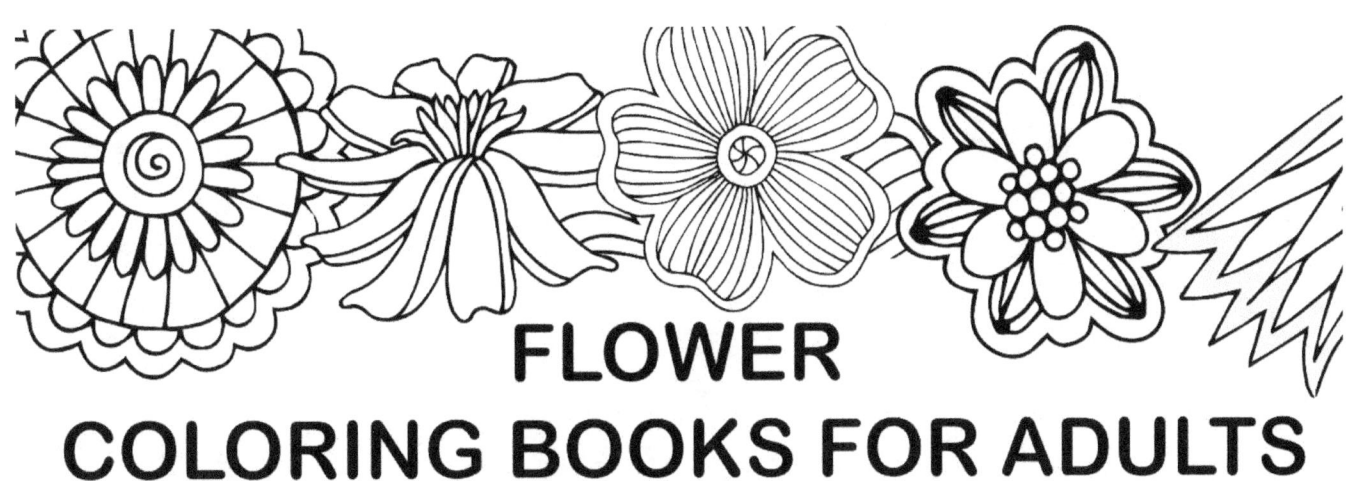

FLOWER
COLORING BOOKS FOR ADULTS

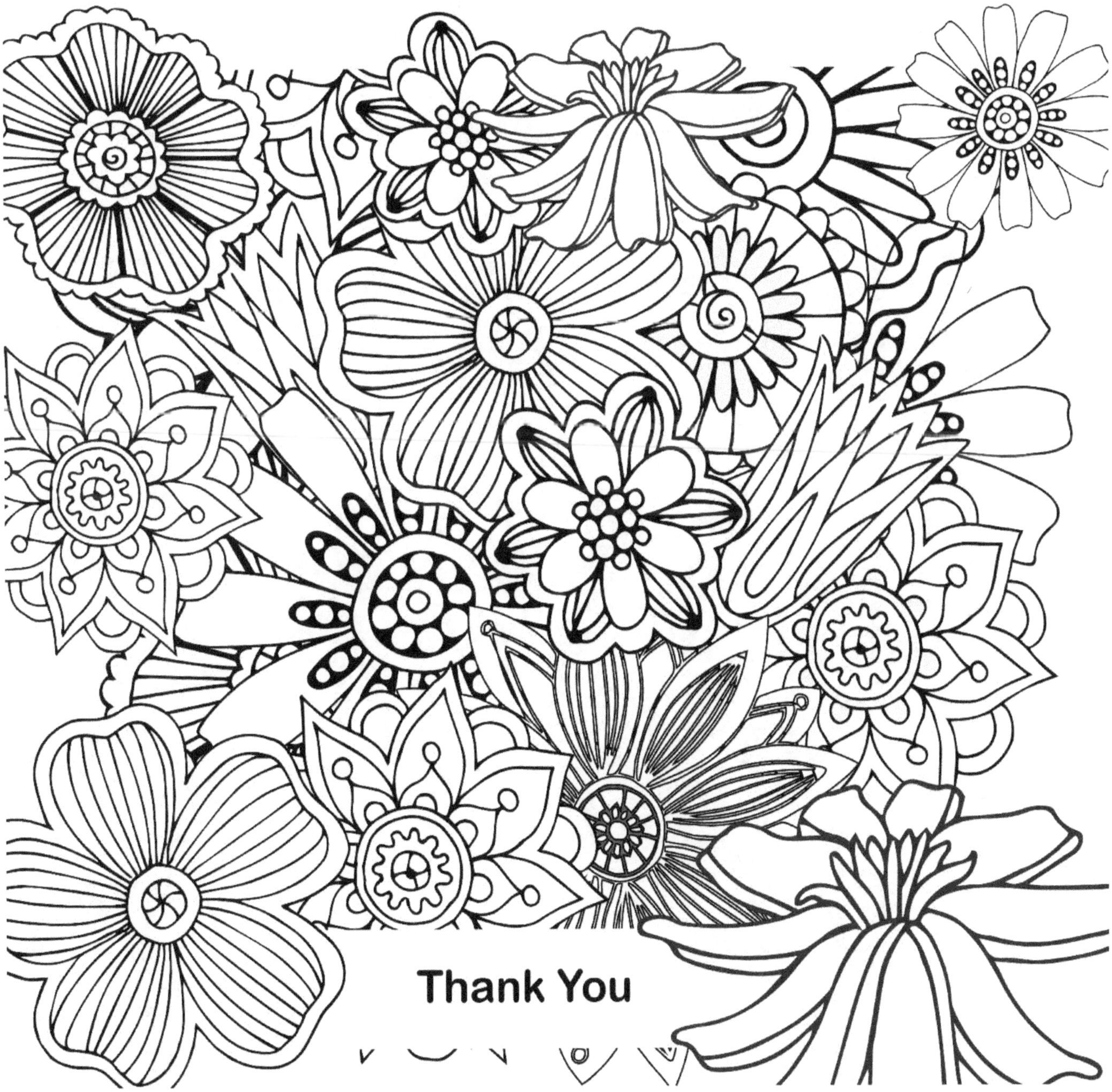

Thank You

www.ingramcontent.com/pod-product-compliance
Lightning Source LLC
Chambersburg PA
CBHW080642180526
45168CB00008B/3279